Praise f

'Caroline Welch's wise and ti... the many roles we play, to bring more presence into our lives each day— not just through meditation, but in a variety of wise ways that lead to a richer, less stressful, more balanced life. Sharing her own experience from both Eastern and Western cultures, she offers a wealth of insight and sage advice about pacing, multitasking, relationships, and other essentials; and, as a result, readers will find themselves thinking in new ways about their own homelife, worklife, and the fine art of simply being in the world.'

—Diane Ackerman, *New York Times* bestselling author of *The Zookeeper's Wife*

'I love this book! It's important that we all embrace the moment, be present, and cherish our time in the here and now. Caroline Welch inspires us to make mindfulness a way of being. The practical steps in this powerful guide lay the groundwork for more calm and less chaos in our lives. What a wonderful way to enhance our health and build a stronger mind!'

—Goldie Hawn, producer, actress, founder of the Hawn Foundation/MindUP, and author of *10 Mindful Minutes*

'A powerful statement of how presence can change our lives. *The Gift of Presence* is a must if you are in a transformational period in your life. Caroline Welch has brilliantly laid out how to live intentionally rather than on autopilot.'

—Diego Perez aka Yung Pueblo, author of *Inward*

'Caroline Welch has gifted us with *The Gift of Presence*—an inviting, accessible, and beautifully written resource for women. Genuine and down-to-earth, Caroline demystifies mindfulness and provides practical suggestions to make it real. A perfect gift for any woman wanting to be more present while juggling the ups and downs of everyday life!'

—Susan Bauer-Wu, PhD, RN, president, Mind & Life Institute, and author of *Leaves Falling Gently*

'Caroline Welch has created a wonderfully accessible discourse on a phenomenon that can benefit all of us. It is impossible to engage meaningfully in the world or effectively with others without first being PRESENT. Receptive awareness is an easy concept but requires evidence-based mindfulness practices to fully actualize in our lives. This book will make a difference to its readers.'

—Drew Pinsky, MD, television host and *New York Times* bestselling
  coauthor of *The Mirror Effect*

'Welch's wonderful book is a mindfulness guide for women of all ages. Her gentle, practical, and profound guidance reflects her great insight into the minds and hearts of women.'

—Mary Pipher, PhD, *New York Times* bestselling author of *Reviving
  Ophelia* and *Women Rowing North*

'Caroline Welch makes a very compelling case for the power of mindfulness to positively transform our lives as women. She deftly navigates the scientific and theoretical foundations of mindfulness while offering a beautiful invitation to become more mindful without ever veering into self-help jargon. *The Gift of Presence* may be written for women, but it is truly a universal guide for anyone interested in strengthening and deepening their relationships, becoming more effective in reaching their goals, and having more joyful and meaningful lives.'

—B. Natterson-Horowitz, MD, visiting professor, Department of
  Human Evolutionary Biology, Harvard University, professor of
  Medicine/Cardiology, UCLA, and *New York Times* bestselling author
  of *Zoobiquity* and *Wildhood*

'This beautifully written book about presence invites women to connect with what is most meaningful in life. It offers practical tools for mindful living that anyone can adopt. It is infused with down-to-earth wisdom, relatable stories, and a look at the science behind it all. Highly recommended!'

—Diana Winston, director of Mindfulness Education at UCLA's Mindful
  Awareness Research Center and author of *The Little Book of Being*

'What a welcome resource Caroline Welch's mindfulness guide is for us—the rich array of stories, teachings, and examples lovingly gathered here touch all of our lives. Rigorous research is presented clearly in a strong yet gentle voice. *The Gift of Presence* is a unique contribution that will benefit countless women—and men, too.'

—Trudy Goodman, PhD, founding teacher at InsightLA

'This is a wonderfully useful tool for helping women to find peace and calm in the midst of busy lives. Highly accessible yet filled with the latest cutting-edge science, this book will teach you how to use presence as a pathway to happiness.'

—Kristin Neff, PhD, associate professor, University of Texas at
   Austin, and author of *Self-Compassion: The Proven Power of Being
   Kind to Yourself*

'Calling all women! At a time when we are juggling more than ever before, our stress levels are not just increasing, but have reached levels that are 40 percent greater than men's. Taking care of ourselves has never been more important, and Caroline Welch provides a research-based, healthy path to living with presence and purpose that can make a lasting difference on our health and well-being starting now.'

—Jennifer Siebel Newsom, first partner of California, filmmaker,
   advocate, and mother of four

'We live in a world of culturally constructed messages—often disempowering for women—that shape our beliefs, behaviors, and sense of self. *The Gift of Presence* is the antidote. Caroline Welch masterfully blends science, stories, and practices, offering doable ways to be our most resilient selves and get through even the toughest of times.'

—Michelle Reugebrink, firefighter, Mindfulness and Resiliency Program
   manager, and Forest Therapy guide and coach

'An evocative reminder that arriving at presence and purpose in your life is as close as your next breath . . . and that's when things get interesting.

Caroline Welch has provided us with a wonderful guide for finding and harnessing these life-transforming qualities.'

—Zindel Segal, PhD, professor, University of Toronto, and author of
    The Mindful Way Through Depression

'This is a lovely book, scholarly, inviting and wise. From her own fascinating journey, plus the stories of women she's interviewed and taught, Caroline Welch brings us a fresh and user-friendly synthesis of the benefits of meditation and how to make them ours. She weaves a tapestry of memorable concepts, scientific insights, and practical tips on how to live a more mindful life. By enhancing our receptivity to moments of presence that grace our lives, we can make mindful awareness the foundation for an ever-richer life of connection, compassion, and joy.'

—Diana Chapman Walsh, president emerita, Wellesley College,
    trustee emerita, Amherst College, Massachusetts Institute of
    Technology, and Mind and Life Institute

'*The Gift of Presence* is a gift for us all—filled with practical insights and fascinating science about the power of mindfulness. By interviewing more than 100 women from diverse backgrounds, Caroline Welch has gathered real-life examples of how being present enriches our lives, allows us to find purpose and meaning, to recharge and renew ourselves, and to pivot when we need to course-correct. Inspiring, well-written, and wise, it's a must-read for women of all ages.'

—Arianna Huffington, founder and CEO, Thrive Global

'It's so easy to forget what matters and race through our decades. Caroline Welch's wise and clear book shows us how mindful awareness can give us back our life. This fresh and entirely accessible guide explores cultivating presence through formal practice and throughout the moments of your day. It will help you reconnect to your true purpose, call forth your inner resourcefulness, and awaken the fullness of your heart.'

—Tara Brach, author of *Radical Acceptance* and *Radical Compassion*

'This is an important, eye-opening book for anyone who wants to understand women who feel stressed out, who feel that they must still do more for less, that they and their work are devalued in a world where glass ceilings still abound. With clarity and the testimony of over 100 women she has worked with, author Caroline Welch offers pragmatic mindfulness exercises to discover one's purpose in life, to summon the courage to change direction if necessary, to set priorities, and to let go of what simply can't get done in order to cultivate inner peace and harmony.'

—Sharon Salzberg, author of *Lovingkindness* and *Real Happiness*

'In this inspiring guide, Caroline Welch synthesizes cutting-edge science and contemplative wisdom from across cultures and walks of life, drawing from her own remarkable, yet relatable life and the experiences of dozens of women. Reading this book is an immersion in a relaxing yet rejuvenating retreat, providing a map for greater presence and deeper purpose in our lives. *The Gift of Presence* is one of the most precious and lasting gifts you can give to yourself.'

—Elissa Epel, PhD, professor, University of California San Francisco,
and *New York Times* bestselling coauthor of *The Telomere Effect*

'If you have an ongoing mindfulness practice and especially if you—like me—do not, Caroline Welch's *The Gift of Presence* is the book you didn't know you needed. It gives you answers to questions you didn't know you had. It's like a cup of tea with a friend on a rainy afternoon—a very wise, gentle, informed friend. You simply walk away feeling better, glad to have it in your life and looking forward to opening it again and again.'

—Sally Field, actor and author of *In Pieces*

'Caroline Welch offers us a timely prescription for vitality and resilience for women—and men—in an age of distraction, providing a scientifically sound and accessible path to clarity in our busy lives. A nutritious menu of mind-strengthening tools, this accessible guide harnesses the research findings of how being present with open awareness can transform your medical health and even slow the aging process. Take these practical steps to live with presence and purpose in your life, creating the wellness you deserve.'

—Mark Hyman, MD, head of Strategy and Innovation, Cleveland Clinic Center for Functional Medicine, and *New York Times* bestselling author of *Food: What the Heck Should I Eat?* and *Food: What the Heck Should I COOK?*

'There is a simple, heartfelt invitation here, calling to you through Caroline and so many women's voices. In *The Gift of Presence,* you will find permission and support for what matters. You can be flexible, inspired, grateful, kind to yourself, present and wise.'

—Jack Kornfield, author of *A Path with Heart*

'I am always looking for that one book that can help a regular, busy person understand and develop a practice of presence, mindfulness, and heartful living. I found it in Caroline Welch's *The Gift of Presence.* If you are the kind of woman (or man, for that matter) who isn't prepared to enter a monastery or even go on a short retreat, this book will be a valued resource at work and home—a guide to forging a peaceful, warm, and kind relationship with yourself and your world.'

—Elizabeth Lesser, cofounder of Omega Institute and *New York Times* bestselling author of *Broken Open*

The Gift of Presence

CAROLINE WELCH is the CEO and cofounder, with Dr. Dan Siegel, of the Mindsight Institute in Santa Monica, California. A graduate of the University of Wisconsin Law School with a master's degree from the University of Southern California, she started her career in law as a corporate litigator. Welch has served as a Los Angeles County court-appointed mediator, as well as in-house counsel at MGM Studios and Spelling Entertainment Group. She began her mindfulness practice forty years ago while working in Japan as an English teacher. Welch provides lectures and workshops to enhance well-being in our personal and professional lives. She and her husband, Dan, live in Santa Monica with their dog, Charlie, and have two adult children.

The Gift of Presence

a mindfulness guide for women

CAROLINE WELCH

SCRIBE
Melbourne • London

Scribe Publications
2 John Street, Clerkenwell, London, WC1N 2ES, United Kingdom
18–20 Edward St, Brunswick, Victoria 3056, Australia

Published by arrangement with TarcherPerigee, an imprint of Penguin
Publishing Group, a division of Penguin Random House LLC

Published by Scribe 2020

Book design by Elke Sigal

Some names and identifying characteristics have been changed to protect
the privacy of the individuals involved.

Neither the publisher nor the author is engaged in rendering professional
advice or services to the individual reader. The ideas, procedures, and
suggestions contained in this book are not intended as a substitute for
consulting with your physician. All matters regarding your health require
medical supervision. Neither the author nor the publisher shall be liable or
responsible for any loss or damage allegedly arising from any information
or suggestion in this book.

Printed and bound in the UK by CPI Group (UK) Ltd, Croydon CR0 4YY

Scribe Publications is committed to the sustainable use of natural resources
and the use of paper products made responsibly from those resources.

9781913348106 (UK edition)
9781925849998 (Australian edition)
9781925938289 (ebook)

Catalogue records for this book are available from the National Library of
Australia and the British Library.

scribepublications.co.uk
scribepublications.com.au

For Madeleine, Elizabeth, Lisa, and Sue

CONTENTS

INTRODUCTION

As I was rushing through the airport to catch a flight, phone in one hand, handbag over my shoulder, trying hard not to spill my coffee as I maneuvered through the early-morning crowds, the cover of a magazine showing an elephant teetering on an exercise ball caught my eye. I only read the first two words of the headline: "Forget balance . . . ," but that was all I needed to see. I stopped to buy the magazine. It turned out to be the *Harvard Business Review*. What was it about those two words—"forget balance"—that made me feel calm, peaceful, and deeply relieved? After thinking about it for a few minutes, I realized that I was constantly swimming upstream to attain some magical balance in my life, both personally and professionally. The prospect of abandoning the search felt freeing. After all, balance suggests a state of equilibrium between two things. But who has just two things to balance in life?

As women of all ages and stages are called upon to play more and more roles, we often feel overwhelmed, on edge, and depleted. Most of us serve as command central for multiple life domains. We have *more tasks than time, which means more juggling than balancing*. Simultaneous demands and high expectations—imposed not only by others but also by ourselves—have led to pervasive multitasking and our ongoing, futile quest for balance—all of which are exhausting us.

Is there anything that can help make us be more calm and less chaotic? More at ease and less burdened? More focused and less distracted? Are there some things that we might already be doing and ways of being that are important for us to continue for our well-being? The answer is a resounding "Yes!" The mental state of Presence can provide exactly what we need in our lives.

Presence is a calm, clear, open, receptive state of mind that can also simply be called *mindfulness* or *mindful awareness*. It's being aware by paying attention to what's going on as it's happening without getting carried away by our judgments or opinions. Presence is a free, natural resource that is available to us anywhere and at any time. No special equipment is required. Being more mindful or present can create many research-established enhancements in our lives, from our medical health to our relationships. Presence can reduce stress and build resilience. When we are present, we are mindfully aware of life's ups and downs, strengthening our ability to not only handle difficulties, but also be more joyful.

Mindfulness embodies a dynamic, active process of growth and change, a way of being present in order to make informed and effective choices when it comes to embracing the many and diverse yet interconnected dimensions of our physical, mental, and social well-being.

Take a moment to consider how it would be for you to . . .

be on autopilot less often.

say the right thing at the right time more often.

be empowered to say no without guilt.

spend less time in unhelpful thought loops.

Believe it or not, these are all within your reach. We'll be discussing how being present can, over time, become our default way of being, more and more often.

Here's an example of Presence applied to your everyday life: Think of a time when you said the wrong thing and you knew it as soon as you spoke the words. We've all had this experience. Words once expressed can't be taken back. But what if you could take a split-second before acting to respond, rather than just react? Think of it as placing a tiny but powerful buffer between the trigger of what was said to you and your response. It's the difference between blurting something out reactively and responding mindfully.

I wrote this book with the intention of making the *why* and the *how* of mindfulness clear, accessible, and sustainable for anyone wondering, "How is this ever going to fit into my busy life?" The short answer is that it's not going to *fit* into your life, or sit at the bottom of your to-do list, but rather that mindfulness can become a way of being, a way of life, a state of mind, that will infuse more and more moments of each day. You'll likely be relieved to know that being mindfully aware does not mean more goals to meet or standards to live up to. I'm not adding more to what's expected of you but rather offering a different way of approaching what's already facing you each day that ultimately can make a difference, so that you can feel more peaceful, more on top of it more often, or at least "gainin' on it," as my dad used to say. You can begin to feel calmer and more grounded, any place and any time—as soon as today. Everything in this book is an invitation, not an expectation.

One thing I've learned over the past twelve years of working at the Mindsight Institute and offering mindfulness workshops for women is that many of us are aware of the benefits of mindfulness, and may even have had a mindfulness practice, such as yoga or meditation, for a few weeks, months, or even years, but then life got in the way and that was the end of the practice. Whether you are unfamiliar with or new to mindfulness, had a practice at one time but couldn't sustain it, feel guilty for not having one, or aspire to deepen your practice, this book invites you to make small changes that can lead to big impacts. Just as when we're getting settled in a cozy, oversized chair, a slight adjustment can make a huge difference.

My own journey with mindfulness began over forty years ago when I was working as an English teacher in Hiroshima, Japan. One of my students introduced me to a small temple nearby called Buttsu-ji where I started to attend weekend retreats. I couldn't understand much of what little instruction there was in Japanese, but I did over the next three years come to treasure the inner peace and quiet I experienced during my visits, which involved sitting in silence on a tatami mat, as still as possible, in the long, chilly meditation hall for one to two hours at a time and doing various tasks around the grounds of the temple. I could not have imagined then how mindfulness would not only become so popular in the United States and throughout the world, but also come back into my life and play such a prominent role, both personally and professionally. While working as a corporate litigator, for example, my mindfulness practice was the one thing that I could rely on to keep me centered and (mostly) confident that I could handle whatever the day might bring.

I became curious about how we cultivate mindfulness and apply it in our everyday lives, so I interviewed more than one hundred women from diverse backgrounds to try to understand its impact throughout the course of their lives. From their powerful stories, a pattern emerged in which I noticed that Presence played a key role in their well-being and was evident in three aspects of their lives: Purpose, Pivoting, and Pacing. I came to call these "the 3 Ps." Presence provides the essential starting point, the foundation for all 3 Ps.

The first P, Purpose, is our life's aim, which gives us direction and provides meaning. It's what gets us out of bed in the morning. Like Presence, Purpose is free, and its benefits for our well-being are so extensive that if it were a medication, we would call it a miracle drug. Research shows how powerful having a Purpose is for us at any age—it can add years to our lives, cut the risk of Alzheimer's by more than half, and increase our resiliency, to mention just a few of its major health benefits. These are benefits that we can all enjoy, so we will be exploring how to find and sustain Purpose as we move through our lives.

The second P, Pivoting, offers us the option to make a change when necessary—or even before absolutely necessary—and, as in basketball, keep one foot in place while exploring and determining what's possible. Decision making can be daunting and unsettling as we often fear failure and resist change. However, with Pivoting we are reminded that we have the support of our relationships, experience, and resources before, during, and after making changes. And proactive Pivoting—making a change before we are forced to do so—usually means having more options.

The third P, Pacing, refers not only to the speed at which we live our lives but also the overall trajectory of the many marathons and sprints that we run back to back. No matter our ages or stages, we sometimes feel that we need to figure everything out at once. Through the wider, more nuanced lens of Pacing we can come to realize that we need not do it all, all at once. With a longer view we can come to more readily embrace the life chapter we are in, take time to savor what's present, and welcome new experiences as they arise with our changing life phases.

The women whom I interviewed for this book comprise a diverse group from around the world, ages twenty-three to ninety, representing different demographics, including life stage, ethnicity, race, nationality, employment status, gender identity, and occupation.

I interviewed women like Beyza, a single mom of a teenager who left her "claustrophobic" job in finance for one in a hospital that would "feed her soul"; Melissa, a teacher at her local community college, who led what she called "a less complicated life than most" until she lost her home in a devastating California forest fire; Danielle, who left a demanding career in advertising to raise her three children; Zhang Wei, a psychotherapist who lost not only her brother at a young age but her twin sister when she took her own life as well as the lives of her two children; and Guadalupe, a single mom who works long, unpredictable hours in the clothing industry.

The women also represented various levels of experience with mindfulness, from having a formal, daily mindfulness practice to feeling guilty for not having one, to having no formal but many informal mindfulness practices. Guadalupe, for example, has no formal mindfulness practice, but gave examples of being very present for her life. As she opens her front door upon returning home from work each day, she takes just one breath before she steps into her house. She has found that this seemingly small practice has made it possible for her to be present for her daughter, which has made a huge difference in their relationship.

On more than one occasion during an interview, the interviewee would say something along the lines of "I am the most unmindful person you know." I then thought to myself, *That actually is a very mindful thing to say.* This brings us to one of the main messages of this book. Mindfulness can infuse our everyday life, and it's likely that you are already being present for some, if not several, moments in your day, as was the case with Guadalupe. My hope is for you to come to appreciate the power of those moments over time and build on them as best you can, making Presence a way of life.

Please know I'm a work in progress, just like everyone else. I can't say I don't have hectic days, because I do. For example, I recently missed an event on my calendar and even broke my toe while rushing to the airport (yes, the airport again)! However, when I take time for my mindfulness practice *especially* on those days when I feel I am too busy to do so, I notice the difference. What's different? I feel calmer, more centered. I even feel calmer when I'm surrounded by chaos. I also move through the day bringing my most resilient self forward more often, which means more focus and less reactivity.

For those of us who work long hours at home or in the workplace, who receive unequal pay, are objectified, have unreliable child care, hit a glass ceiling, or feel exasperated at the end of a long day in unenlightened work environments, I'm not saying just be present and all will be well. Presence is not a panacea, not a cure-all for the many challenges we face. I wish I could offer you the power of Panakeia, the Greek goddess of universal healing, but I can't. What I am saying is that while we can't control others or world events, we can control how we choose to respond to what's happening around us—and even within us. And that can allow us to feel more at ease and more in charge of our lives.

I've written this mindfulness guide for women, but of course anyone can benefit from reading it. In fact, even though my workshops and lectures are usually directed to women, there are always a few men in the room. When I've asked the men why they've chosen to attend, they respond along the lines of, "I want to be the best uncle I can be by doing what I can to know the life of my two nieces who are just starting their careers," "I'm a teacher and I want to better understand what's going on with my students," or "I just want to learn more about my partner."

Throughout this book, you will notice (I hope) the representation of a water droplet. In the figure, the vertical, mirrored feature symbolizes the past and the future, and the horizontal feature represents the present or spaciousness. Being in a state of Presence is often described as experiencing spaciousness and equanimity. Whenever you see the water droplet, I invite you to check in with yourself and see if you are present.

Don't be alarmed if you notice the water droplet and realize that you've been ruminating about the past or worrying about the future. Perhaps you are concerned about an email you sent recently or an upcoming deadline. This type of mind-wandering is natural, and in fact, it's to be expected. *We actually spend about half of our waking hours consumed by constant thought loops, most of which are repeats.* When you realize that your focus has wandered, just gently, kindly bring it back to the book—without berating yourself, please! Consider the water droplet a gentle cue to pause and become present— one quick example of an informal, impromptu mindfulness practice. Being present is a skill we can cultivate; just like building any other skill, it takes practice, and that's why we cultivate Presence, mindfulness, or mindful awareness through practices both formal and informal.

The idea is to notice, to become aware, to pay attention, to place your mind and body in the same place at the same time. The water droplet reminds us to inhabit the only moment we have, this one unrepeatable, present moment. Research confirms that being present, as in focusing our minds on what we are currently doing, creates more well-being.

We are all on this journey together to develop the confidence that we can handle whatever comes our way by accessing our most resilient, flexible selves. Let's begin now.

The
Gift *of*
Presence

PART 1

The Power of Presence

We don't need to be perfect or problem-free to be
present for the moment.
—MARY PIPHER

IF YOU'RE LIKE MOST OF US, your thoughts are plentiful, nonstop,
and not necessarily helpful. We lose ourselves continuously in ongoing thought loops that sweep us out of the present moment.
During our average day, most of us speak around 16,000 words, but
our thoughts—our internal, tireless chatterbox minds—produce
tens of thousands more, 95 percent of which are reruns. No wonder
it's so hard to get to our basic stillness; it's buried under tens of thousands of thoughts.

One of the most difficult times to be present is when things are
not going well, and although that's exactly when we need Presence
the most, it's also when it's least available to us. If you're like me you
may tend to catastrophize, which can truly exacerbate the situation.
During a visit to Myanmar, neuropsychiatrist Dan Siegel—my life
partner of more than thirty years and work partner for twelve
years—and I visited the breathtaking, sprawling, 2,500-year-old

Shwedagon Pagoda in Yangon, where dozens of monks gather daily at sunrise to meditate. We entered quietly and selected our spots. I had not been sitting for more than five minutes when a cricket climbed into my ear. I could feel and hear it thrashing around, hitting my outer ear canal as it tried to escape.

My mind raced and my thoughts went something like this: *Oh no, it's our departure day, I'll need to delay my flight, find a doctor, which will be a real challenge, I'm sure the doctor will not have any experience with a case like this, then I'll need a surgeon to remove the cricket, most likely I'll lose my hearing, I can't really see how I can survive this without at least some hearing loss, I just hope I don't get a rare disease . . .* All of this in the span of less than three seconds, although it seemed like fifteen minutes, and then most surprisingly, the cricket left my ear canal on its own. I felt hugely relieved and pretty foolish for having made such an elaborate tale about the dreaded future that was never to be. We easily enter the land of catastrophic thinking where *the worst case is the only case*, facing thoughts and feelings far more elaborate and negative than whatever the initial experience was. I'm sure you can bring to mind your own examples.

No matter our life experiences, our choice of occupation, or our family situation, we tend to review our lives with our *woulda, coulda, shouldas*, in search of a perfect past or at least an improved one. Our minds have a mind of their own and are eager to get on to the next thing, something "better," or to take us back to something that happened in the past. Before you know it, we've lost ourselves in stories, thoughts, or feelings about the future or past. I imagine that you're familiar, as I am, with these thought loops—what I like to call *thought safaris*. We frequently miss completely what's happening right now and generally aren't content with the here and now anyway. We make plans for futures that rarely unfold, either looking ahead to what we imagine will finally bring us the happiness we seek and deserve, or fearing dangers and disasters that may very well never occur. As Mark Twain said, "[I] have known a great many troubles, but most of them never happened."

We can all agree that our nonstop thoughts keep us out of the present moment, so how do we spend more time in the present? That's what we'll be discussing in the first part of this book, starting with defining Presence.

What Is Presence?

Our species has had a word for Presence for hundreds of years. The origin of *presence* dates back to 1300–1500, Middle French, Middle English, and Latin. By dictionary definition, Presence means being with another or "in the immediate vicinity or proximity." The opposite of Presence is absence. The perplexing thing about Presence is that I can be sitting across from you at a meeting (physically seeming present) but actually be absent if my mind is someplace else. This is not a new feature of our human condition, although the prevalence of digital devices has increased the potential that our minds and bodies are not in the same place at the same time.

I'll be using the terms *Presence, mindfulness*, and *mindful awareness* synonymously and interchangeably in this book, adopting the widely embraced definition from Jon Kabat-Zinn: "Mindfulness is awareness, cultivated by paying attention in a sustained and particular way: on purpose, in the present moment, and non-judgmentally." Sometimes Kabat-Zinn adds the phrase "as if your life depended on it" because as he explains, "it does to such a profound extent." Mindfulness teacher Susan Bauer-Wu explains, "When you are mindful, you have emotional balance, with fewer extreme highs and lows, and a sense of spaciousness and inquisitiveness toward whatever arises. *You can catch yourself when your mind is caught in a downward spiral of negative thinking or when other mental obstacles trip you up*" (italics mine).

Presence is a state of "**receptive awareness**" that enables us to **pay attention** to what is happening **right now**. It's more than awareness: it's receptive awareness, or being open to whatever is happening **without getting carried away with our own opinions or judgments** about it, welcoming both good news and bad news **with curiosity and kindness toward ourselves and others**. Please notice that I didn't say *without judgment*, because our minds are judging all of the time; that's what they do. The point is that we aren't trying to get rid of judgments; we are just trying to keep in mind that judgments—like thoughts, memories, and emotions—are simply mental activities that come and go. Without mindfulness, we very quickly—often without even being aware of it—put our opinions or preconceived notions front and center, as we have spent our lives assessing, categorizing, and judging situations, events, the people around us, as well as ourselves.

Even with Presence, we might still sometimes say the wrong thing at the wrong time, feel annoyed when our neighbor's noises wake us up early in the morning, and experience "bad things" in our lives. So, what will be different? Our *relationship* to our feelings and experiences—whether happy, sad, or in between—will shift. *More time spent being present means that more often we can bring forth our most flexible or resilient selves.* We will be less thrown off when life's events emerge. My ninety-year-old mother-in-law, Sue Siegel, describes the difference Presence has made in her life this way: "What used to annoy me, now amuses me."

Imagine that you've just visited a dear friend or family member who has been hospitalized unexpectedly. We've all made those visits. As you finally exit the hospital, Presence can make the difference between being overwhelmed with sadness and feeling slightly better by listening even for a few seconds to the birds chirping, or noticing the first lilacs of spring.

A Wandering Mind Is an Unhappy Mind

As you are reading these words, are you taking in what you are reading or has your mind wandered off? If your mind has wandered off, you are not alone. Psychologists Matthew Killingsworth and Daniel Gilbert studied five thousand people and showed that *about 50 percent of our time is spent thinking about something other than what we are doing.* This means we spend only about half of our time in the present. On top of that, *80 percent of the time we are thinking about something that is actually more stressful than what we are currently doing, meaning we are the authors of the stress we are seeking to avoid.* The researchers also collected data on happiness using a "track your happiness" app to prompt thousands of people to respond to questions about what activity they were engaged in, what they were thinking about, and how happy they were. They found a 47 percent mind-wandering rate, even when respondents were having sex, engaging in conversation, or exercising.

The researchers also found that when we are aware of what we are doing, we are the happiest, regardless of what we are actually doing. In other words, even when we're doing something we find unpleasant or boring, such as paying our bills, we feel calmer when present for the activity rather than when thinking about something else. Our mental and physical well-being is enhanced when we are present for what is happening as it happens, whether it be it boring or exciting, pleasant or unpleasant.

Why are we unhappy when unintentionally mind-wandering? Because when we aren't present, we can easily get stuck in ruminating, reliving, and regretting the past, or fast-forwarding, catastrophizing, and worrying about the future. This unintentional, negative mind-wandering causes us to feel distracted and unhappy. Sound familiar? Also, in high-stress situations we are more prone to unintentional mind-wandering.

You may be thinking, "I actually enjoy daydreaming, reminiscing, and just letting my mind wander. It's relaxing for me." I'm not suggesting that you give up intentional mind-wandering or daydreaming, because when it's *intentional*, it actually supports creativity, positive emotions, insight, and relaxation, and it helps us better plan for the future. Let's say you're a songwriter working on a new song, and you go out for a walk around the block and intentionally let your mind wander in order to enhance your creativity. Or perhaps you've just had a challenging conversation with a family member or work colleague and you go for a run, setting the intention of letting your mind wander, and being open to whatever feelings or thoughts may come up. Allowing ourselves this space can bring insight. As you can see, intentional mind wandering is

Body present 100 percent of the time, but where's your mind?

beneficial in many ways. The key is to be aware of what our intention is.

Seven Key Features of Presence

Now that you have a general sense of what Presence is, it's time to look more closely at its features, and how they unfold in our everyday lives. These features are inspired by the work of mindfulness-based cognitive therapy (MBCT) pioneers John Teasdale, Mark Williams, and Zindel Segal. At the end of each of the seven features, you'll find a quick practice called "**Now is a good time to . . . ,**" which I encourage you to try so that you may experience for yourself what I'm describing.

More Presence Means Less Autopilot

We spend much of our time on autopilot; we walk, eat, commute, and even talk without clear awareness of what we are doing. We're just going through the motions, guided by our routines and habits. Have you ever had the experience of finding yourself following a familiar route to one of your usual destinations and passing right by your intended stop? Or calling one person when you intended to call another? Or perhaps even more troubling, driving along on a city street, suddenly discovering bright, flashing red lights in your rearview mirror, and having no idea how long you've been unaware of them?

These everyday experiences can remind us how rushing through life keeps us from being present. Although we may dismiss such occurrences as inconsequential, unpleasant side effects of our busy lives, they are useful illustrations of the frequent mismatch between where we are physically at any given moment and where our minds are.

It's not easy to pause and be present for more and more moments. Living intentionally rather than automatically means that we can choose what's next rather than remaining entrenched in our habits. Not doing so means missing much of our lives as we rush around on autopilot. Presence brings a fresh lens to our lives, allowing us to see things as if for the very first time, and to reinhabit right now.

Now is a good time to . . . pick one activity you do every day on autopilot and make it a time when you can be fully aware, such as taking a shower and feeling the water on your skin, or driving and feeling your hands on the steering wheel, or—? Notice the difference for yourself. Please be patient, persist, and try it with other activities, too.

More Sensing Means Less Preoccupation with Thinking

We tend to spend a lot of time in our heads, lost in our thoughts, thinking and overthinking things rather than experiencing them directly. This translates for all of us to less time spent in the present. *We think not only about our feelings and sensations—we even think about our thoughts.* Thinking can overpower our ability to sense and feel directly, which often leads us to create our own stressful interpretations of events. For example, my neighbor passed right by me this morning while walking Hamlet, her pet pig, without even saying hello. (Yes, there's a pet pig in our neighborhood . . . it's good to know that you *are* present on the page!). If you and I were sitting around a table with others, it wouldn't be surprising for each one of us to have a different interpretation of what happened with my neighbor. Would you ask yourself: *Do I feel worried that I did some-*

thing wrong? Do I feel sad that she might not like me? Do I feel angry that she ignored me? Do I feel concerned at the possibility that she might have been preoccupied with something else?

A single situation can lead us to a wide range of thoughts and interpretations, and these thoughts and interpretations—rather than the situation itself—shape how we feel. Teasdale, Williams, and Segal explain it this way: *"Our interpretations of events reflect what we bring to them just as much as the reality of the events themselves"* (italics mine).

To make matters even worse, we are often *unaware of our interpretations* of situations, and that's where Presence can be especially useful. When we do find ourselves lost in thinking, we can learn to shift our attention to how we feel in order to try to relate directly to the experience. Unfortunately, the ability to refocus our attention in this way is not a switch we can flip on and off. Managing our attention so that we can directly sense our experiences, rather than just relate to them through our thoughts and judgments, is a skill set that takes time and practice to develop.

Now is a good time to . . . bring to mind a slight, insult, or sadness you have felt recently and have a look at what went through your mind. Did you feel angry, sad, scared, or—? We each have our own "go-to" emotion. Just being aware of what emotion we are experiencing is a solid starting point for living with more Presence.

More Living in the Present Means Less Living in the Past or Future

Being in the present is about *being here*, not *getting there*. I'm wondering if you are present with me on this page right now, or have your thoughts whisked you off to your dinner plans or the movie you saw last night? Pioneer in modern memory research Endel Tulving calls this process by which we look at our past, present, and prospective future *mental time travel*. It's one of our brain's unique characteristics, and is thought to be one of the features that distinguishes us from other mammals. It's pretty amazing that we can travel to different times and places in our minds, actually feeling that we are in the past or present. *Mental time travel serves us well only when it's used to plan for the future and learn from the past; it's beneficial to have thoughts about our past and future as part of our present experience.*

With Presence, we can have thoughts about the past or present, but we experience them with intention, as part of our present experience. When helpful, these reflections can enhance our lives, rather than detract from them. However, ruminating about the past can mean reexperiencing the pain of past losses, while worrying about the future can mean dreading things that very well may never occur. Examples include replaying in our minds the job interview we are certain we messed up or worrying about how our teen will ever get into college.

Another downside of not being present is missing out on what's going on around us. Let's use FOMO (fear of missing out) in our favor here and reframe it to motivate us to avoid MOON (missing out on now). Furthermore, when we are not present, we are most likely heading into a downward spiral full of negativity. As psychologist Rick Hanson points out in *Buddha's Brain*, we all have a negativity bias; that is, even when of equal intensity, thoughts or emotions of a more negative nature have a greater effect on our psychological state and processes than do neutral or positive things. *Simply stated: Positive things have less impact on our behavior than things that are equally emotional but negative.* The reason for this negativity bias is that it helps us to survive if we err on the side of overestimating the negative so we don't miss a potentially life-threatening aspect of what's going on. Endlessly reexperiencing the pain of our past failures and future worries is both exhausting and stressful, even though it is rooted in our survival history as a species. Unfortunately, the more we dwell on the negative, the more our brains become accustomed to dwelling on the negative and continue to do so.

Have you ever noticed that the past and future change every time you think of them? Each time we think back on a past event, our minds pull up a newly refreshed yet old memory, now shaped by our experiences during the time that has passed since both the event itself occurred and we were last aware of it. Similarly, our imagined future is also always changing, depending on our experiences. As Yogi Berra once observed, "The future ain't what it used to be."

Now is a good time to . . . try it out for yourself. The next time you become aware that your thoughts are focused on the past or present, take a moment to look at them—are they negative, repetitive, and about you? Each of us has one or two habitual thought loops that we find ourselves returning to when we aren't present. The first step is becoming aware, pausing for this present moment we call now. Adding just a few more moments of being present today can make a difference in bringing your most resilient self forward more often.

More Acceptance and Receptivity Means Less Aversion and Reactivity

We all share a deeply ingrained habit of aversion—avoiding, escaping, and trying to get rid of things that we experience as unpleasant or uncomfortable—which not only keeps us out of the present moment but doesn't help us deal at all with what we're trying to avoid. Aversion is hardwired in us, dating back millions of years to a time when we had to avoid things in the outside world such as ferocious animals and forest fires.

When our deeper brain networks, sometimes referred to as our "reptilian brain," senses danger and activates a neural response to help us get ready to fight, flee, freeze, or faint, our prefrontal cortex—the higher brain area associated with executive functioning and rational top-down decision making—can be taken offline. This is sometimes called flying off the handle, flipping your lid, or taking the low road, as our deeper brain networks take over our behavior as they try to help us survive. Our brain's ability to make quick decisions has been historically necessary to keep us safe. Research professor Brené Brown uses the story of a bear charging and asks: "Should I stop, get curious, and wonder if it's a vegan bear?" As she explains, in a life-or-death situation there's no time for questions, and this is why exploring our own emotions, and being open and curious can sometimes be deceptively difficult.

So, what's an appropriate modern-day response to aversion? The answer is to "name it to tame it": to recognize it for what it is, name it, allow it to be present, don't engage, don't resist, and then pay attention to how it affects our mind and body. We don't have to fix it or get rid of it but just see it for what it is. The core of our continued challenge is to not allow our deep-seated tendencies to overrule us but rather to regulate our behavior from a place of Presence. It's the difference between reacting and responding.

You may be thinking, "Why should I welcome bad news, pain, and disappointment?" After all, don't we all prefer to receive good news? Why not focus on the positive in life and just ignore the negative? Doesn't it make sense to avoid unpleasant experiences? No, because that doesn't work well in the long run since our emotions live within us. We can't avoid them. In fact, aversion makes them worse; the more we engage with them and try to push them away, the more we become exhausted and generate even more unpleasant feelings.

The next time you are feeling an unpleasant emotion, start by observing and being curious about your feeling without letting it overcome you and without trying to stop it. Noticing an emotion that is arising, and not identifying with it as the whole of who you are, can empower you to label it as you let it be, not trying to get rid of it or to cling to it. The spaciousness of your awareness as you focus attention on the emotion at that moment can allow it to arise, and then move along as you stay fully in the present. Just inviting the feeling in, naming it, and observing it unfold can be very helpful in changing your relationship with the emotion itself. Exploring our challenges with kindness and curiosity, rather than pushing them away, offers a perfect opportunity for some self-compassion, as it can increase our ability to intentionally take a breath so we can respond rather than react with aversion.

What if you do your best to accept and allow an unpleasant feeling and it just won't go away? It lingers, continues to gnaw at you, and you begin to worry that it will never leave you alone. We each experience aversion with varying physical sensations: tightness; bracing; tension in the face, shoulders, or other body parts. And all of these sensations themselves feel unpleasant. Here are a couple of facts that may help you when you are experiencing such a negative thought safari. First, what do you think the life span of an emotion is? You may be surprised to learn that even a very unpleasant emotion typically lasts *no longer than ninety seconds*—unless we try to chase it away or engage with it, in which case it persists.

Second, *we aren't actually trying to change our feelings; we are trying to change our relationship to them*—that is, the way we hold them in our awareness—to let go of the aversion so that we can be more likely to respond rather than react. This concept is at the heart of Presence. Although we have no control over the challenges that go along with our being human and that will inevitably visit us during our lifetimes, we do have control over how we respond to life's challenges. Psychologist Shauna Shapiro explains, "It's not that we can be happy or feel loving all the time; it's about paying kind attention, and holding anger with kindness, for example." Presence helps us to build a new relationship to challenges, to replace aversion and reactivity with receptivity, and to respond with natural interest, openness, and curiosity toward all experience—whether pleasant, unpleasant, or neither. In this way, we won't remain stuck in the same old habits, and we can take control of our own happiness by taking control of how we choose to respond to life's challenges.

 Now is a good time to . . . pick one unpleasant feeling that keeps coming up for you. Remember, starting slow works well with mindfulness practices. So select something you can likely manage—let's say on a scale of one to ten, it's a three or four. Instead of pushing it away, just observe it, name it, get curious about it. Notice if it starts to last less time and feel like it has less of a hold on you when you neither engage with it nor push it away. Repeat as needed.

More Accepting and Letting Be Means Less Judging

Many mindfulness teachers use the phrase "Accept things as they are," but I appreciate that Teasdale, Williams, and Segal add one important word to that familiar phrase. They say: "Accept things as they *already* are." The addition of *already* sounds final to me, as in "nothing can be done," and that in and of itself somehow helps me be more accepting of whatever I may be facing, and less likely to dwell on what I think should be. It's important to add here that being more accepting does not include enduring abusive relationships or situations. Accepting means allowing ourselves to see with more clarity as we let go of the judging filters that can distort our ability to see the truth of what actually is.

Presence is *accepting what is*, not *striving to make things different*. Once we accept, and access our own essential nature, change follows. Not the other way around. In other words, you are not inadequate. You have all that you need to be present right now. It is a matter of accepting the invitation to be present, not putting another expectation on yourself to be better or different. Even a few seconds of being present can make us feel more in charge of our lives, calmer and better able to respond, rather than react, to life as it comes at us with its dazzling speed. More Presence means being open to a wider array of experience.

Now is a good time to . . . bring to mind some situation that you would love to be able to change but cannot. Each time you think about it, say to yourself, "Let it be." Accept it. Repeat as needed and see what happens. Patience and persistence are especially important here since many of us have a hearty tendency to try to fix and change things.

The Guest House

....

This being human is a guest house.
Every morning a new arrival.

A joy, a depression, a meanness,
some momentary awareness comes

as an unexpected visitor.
Welcome and entertain them all!
Even if they're a crowd of sorrows,
who violently sweep your house
empty of its furniture,

still, treat each guest honorably.
He may be clearing you out
for some new delight.

The dark thought, the shame, the malice,
meet them at the door laughing,
and invite them in.

Be grateful for whoever comes,
because each has been sent
as a guide from beyond.

—JALAL AL-DIN RUMI

Presence Enables Us to Experience Thoughts as More Fleeting and Less Fixed

Our thoughts can feel very real. When we are not in a state of Presence, we tend to overidentify with them, often considering them to be synonymous with *reality* or *me*, to our peril. We lose the perspective that they are simply products of our mind, and we treat our thoughts and ideas about things as if they are absolute truths. They aren't. They may be true, but not necessarily.

Author Byron Katie urges her students to examine their thoughts with four basic questions:

1. Is it true?

2. Can you absolutely know that it's true?

3. How do you react when you believe that thought?

4. Who would you be without the thought?

Katie puts it this way: "I discovered that when I believed my thoughts, I suffered, but that when I didn't believe them, I didn't suffer, and that this is true for every human being . . . I found that suffering is optional."

UCLA researcher Susan Smalley and mindfulness teacher Diana Winston, in their book *Fully Present*, offer this helpful analogy when it comes to Presence as a way of separating or disentangling ourselves from our thoughts: "You can create them, but you do not need to become them. Think about the way a camera works. It 'sees' everything that happens within the frame of the picture, but it is not affected by anything it focuses on. The camera can take any image and simply frame it—just as you can learn to do with your thoughts."

Over time we can learn to relate to our thoughts for what they are: fleeting mental events that are constructions of the mind. Given how much time we spend thinking and overthinking, it's easy to feel that *we are our thoughts*. What would relating to our thoughts as mental events that simply come and go look like in our lives? Imagine having the skill to just observe your thoughts and realize they are not you. Yes, they are products of your mind, and your mind is just a part of you, not all of you.

Meditation teacher Sharon Salzberg describes our tendency to identify more with our mental life—our thoughts and emotions—

than our bodies this way. For example, we may say, "I am sad," or "I am a sad person," not "I am feeling sad." We don't overidentify with our bodies by saying, "I am a sore elbow," but rather we say, "I have a sore elbow" or "my elbow feels sore." When we overidentify with an emotion, as in "the emotion is me," it can take us over and keep us stuck in our familiar ruminations and worries. Just as our thoughts are fleeting mental events, so are our emotions.

Feelings are powerful influences that shape our frame of mind, which in turn shape our patterns of thinking. Patterns of thought often reflect emotional themes similar to the feelings that gave rise to them in the first place. In other words, sad feelings lead to sad thoughts and happy feelings lead to happy thoughts. Each time we are able to recognize a thought as a thought when it arises, register its content, assess its accuracy and hold on us, let it go and come back to our awareness (which is distinct from the thought itself), we can strengthen our Presence or mindful awareness.

 Now is a good time to . . . make a mental note for the next time you are experiencing an emotion such as sadness, to try to free yourself from overidentifying with the emotion by saying to yourself, "I feel sad," rather than "I am sad." See if you can notice or feel the difference when viewing your emotions, thoughts, and memories as fleeting, not fixed.

More Awareness of Broader Needs Means Less Tunnel Vision

We can become hyperfocused on pursuing highly ambitious goals or plans, with a kind of tunnel vision, at a high cost to both ourselves and the people around us. We often exhaust ourselves and become depleted, ignoring certain parts of our lives, and even giving up activities that would nourish us in order to pursue a goal that seems more important. I know that this is a tricky one, because most of us undertake major projects or set demanding goals in the various facets of our lives. I'm not saying that it isn't healthy to have goals; how else could we get anything done? However, the point is to be aware that pursuing ambitious goals can tend to consume us and inevitably at times it feels like they have taken over our entire lives—because they have.

Prioritizing goal attainment over being sensitive to our broader needs often means that we are compromising our health and well-being. So while we pursue a goal that's meaningful to us, how can we reconcile its demands and at the same time pay attention to other aspects of our lives? It isn't easy. In fact, that's what this book is about—how to include in our lives the people and the things that are important to us without becoming overwhelmed and drained. Sometimes family or work demands put us in predicaments that do require our full attention for days or weeks. In these situations, it can be helpful to look at the larger picture, as we'll be doing in Part 4 on Pacing. The basic question with Pacing, as it relates to our pursuing a demanding goal, is whether this is the time to do so—to the extent that we have control over that. With our engaged lives, inevitably projects and goals will sometimes consume us, but keeping in mind our broader view can help us get through such intense times. For now, the important takeaway is that Presence provides the tiny but necessary first step in our becoming aware of when we have become consumed by a particular goal, to the exclusion of our own health and well-being.

Now is a good time to . . . bring to mind something that feels like it has taken over your life, likely because it has. Is there anything you can do to reduce its role in your life right now, or in the near future? Even small adjustments may relieve some of the pressure you feel. Also considering how attaining this goal fits into the broader view of your life can be helpful as you navigate this particularly demanding time.

The Science Supporting the Benefits of Presence

The science underlying the benefits of mindfulness is growing exponentially. In the 1970s, there were just a handful of scientific articles on meditation; today there are approximately seven thousand, with over one thousand released annually. The arrival of the research coincides with neuroscientific findings showing that mindfulness has an impact on the structure and function of our brain through a process called *neuroplasticity*. *Neuro* refers to our neurons, and *plasticity* describes our brain's malleability in response to experience. That is, our adult brain can be transformed by experience. As recently as twenty-five years ago, we believed that after puberty our brain did not change.

Neurons are the basic brain cells that connect with each other at linkages called synapses that help form the structure of the brain. Where we focus our attention, neurons fire, and where this neural firing happens, we grow connections; in areas without firing neurons, we actually can reduce the number of connections, in a process scientists call "synaptic pruning."

Thanks to neuroplasticity, our brain's structure can change with experience, growing our neural connections in the same way that we sculpt our muscles. What does this mean for mindfulness?

It means that the more we can inhabit a mental state of Presence, the more likely the state of brain-firing associated with Presence will become a trait of baseline brain activity that will be activated over time. Under pressure, for example, there is more of a chance that we will be able to inhabit a state of Presence since we have trained that state to be our baseline trait.

So whether we are being fully present for a conversation or practicing yoga, we can create *states that actually become enduring traits.* In other words, we can change our baseline state or habitual pattern— what we tend to do when on autopilot—from a tendency to mindlessly react to a stronger likelihood that we will be able to mindfully respond. In this way, we can come to often respond in ways that may be more consistent with what we really want to say or do rather than what we may blurt out without the benefit of consciously choosing our words. More good news: Our brain's ability to form new connections, and therefore new habits, is possible at any age— with an exponential growth in scientific research specifically around the ways the brain grows with mindfulness practices and their implications for our well-being.

What's the process in the brain by which the state of Presence can become a trait? The idea is that by practicing mindfulness meditation—as in strengthening our focus of attention and opening our awareness, for example—neurons fire and create a clear and receptive state of mind, which when repeated over time can become a trait. Traits occur with the growth of neural connections. The three ways we can strengthen neural connections are by growing new neurons (at least in the hippocampus, but other areas are still being explored), modifying synaptic connections, and laying down myelin (a sheath that makes the communication among interconnected neurons three thousand times faster and more coordinated). Neuroscientist Carla Shatz has paraphrased researcher Donald Hebb's hypothesis about neuroplasticity this way: *Neurons that fire together wire together.* Here is the process as it relates to attention from Dan Siegel's book *Aware*:

> *Where attention goes*
> *Neural firing flows, and*
> *Neural connection grows.*

Just a few minutes of daily meditation provides benefits, and recent studies confirm that the more hours you practice, the greater the benefits. As Goleman and Davidson point out, "At the highest levels of practice we find true altered traits—changes in the brain that science has never observed before, but which we proposed decades ago."

There's one part of the brain that I'd like to introduce now because it made a powerful difference in how I approach my own mindfulness practice. As we've been discussing, the mind naturally wanders, and in fact, it does so by default. Studies have shown that when people are asked to do nothing in an fMRI scanner while their brain activity is being measured, they default to mind-wandering that often takes the form of an ongoing narrative all about themselves. The brain scans of the participants reveal that a large midline network in the cortex lights up, indicating a major increase in neural activity, even though the volunteers had been asked to do nothing inside the scanner. This was the result of excessive activity of the mostly midline circuits of a part of the brain scientists have aptly named the *default mode network* (DMN). Neuroscientist Judson Brewer points out that while the exact functions of the DMN are still debated, given its prominence in self-referential processing, we can think of it as the "me" network that links ourselves to our inner and outer worlds. The DMN's circuits when overactive not only tend to make us self-preoccupied, but as part of our social brain, they cause us to compare ourselves to others and even worry about what others think of us. Imagine for a moment how activated our midline default circuits must be when we visit social media platforms!

Science suggests that one way we can get our chatterbox mind to calm down is to activate the lateral or side sensory regions. For example, when we sense our breath we activate our side or lateral circuits, and the midline DMN where our thought safaris originate quiets down. In brief, activating the lateral sensory circuits inhibits the firing of the midline DMN circuits. As discussed above, over time this intentionally created state of Presence can become a baseline trait, a default way of being. Neuroplasticity enables the connections in the brain to grow, supporting a more balanced or integrated role of the DMN with the rest of our brain. The DMN, for example, is needed for empathy and insight. Having a more integrated DMN means being able to actively choose when to be in the present moment or to focus attention on the past or future. Presence means being able to choose how and where to intentionally focus our attention—in this moment of present sensations, on memories of the past, or on images about the future.

Why am I so excited about the DMN? Because when we are present with our current sensations, our stories starring each one of us are not as likely to take us over. *The two cannot exist simultaneously.* Of course, distractions can still arise; but over time with Presence, when they do arise, we can more readily bring our attention back to the present. Remember, mindfulness is not about an empty mind but a clear mind. Sometimes an overly active and non-integrated DMN can make us anxious, depressed, and even lose touch with who we truly are. More moments experienced in Presence means more time as our most resilient selves. Derek Walcott articulates this concept beautifully in his poem below.

Love After Love

....

The time will come
when, with elation
you will greet yourself arriving
at your own door, in your own mirror
and each will smile at the other's welcome,

and say, sit here. Eat.
You will love again the stranger who was yourself.
Give wine. Give bread. Give back your heart
to itself, to the stranger who has loved you

all your life, whom you ignored
for another, who knows you by heart.
Take down the love letters from the bookshelf,

the photographs, the desperate notes,
peel your own image from the mirror.
Sit. Feast on your life.

—DEREK WALCOTT

Self-Compassion Toward Our Inner Critic

There's nothing inherently troubling about our inner voice or narrative; however, when it's inflexible or negative, as when we ruminate about the past or worry about the future, it can quickly become our inner critic. Are you your own inner critic, or ally? If you are like many of us, you are both, but leaning closer toward inner enemy more often than not.

One of the hardest challenges for us can be to give ourselves a break when we haven't met expectations, either those of others or our own. As a result, befriending or softening our inner enemy can be especially hard work. This is where self-compassion comes in. Researcher Kristin Neff, a pioneer in the field, identifies three core components of self-compassion, which are conceptually distinct but overlap and give rise to one another:

1. Self-kindness, or being understanding with ourselves rather than critical and judgmental;

2. Common humanity, or feeling connected with others and recognizing that imperfection and difficulties are shared parts of our human experience rather than feeling isolated by our shortcomings;

3. Mindfulness, or holding our experiences in awareness rather than avoiding or exaggerating our pain.

Here's how the three components complement each other and are interwoven: The open and accepting stance of mindfulness can assist us in being kind to ourselves by lessening self-judgment. This stance also provides insight so we can recognize our common humanity, realizing that we are all connected and all have challenges. Similarly, self-kindness can lessen the impact of negative emotional experiences so it's easier to be mindful of them, or hold them in our awareness. Furthermore, remembering that we all experience personal failures, which are part of being human, helps lessen self-blame and harsh self-judgment.

WHAT I CAN DO IS ALL I CAN DO AND THAT WILL BE ENOUGH

Neff has experienced the power of self-compassion, not only in her empirical research and teaching thousands of people to be more self-compassionate, but personally, as well. When her son Rowan was diagnosed with autism, she practiced self-compassion, and experienced feelings of disappointment, fear, anxiety, and not knowing if she could cope—all feelings she described as ones "you aren't supposed to have as a parent, let's face it." She allowed herself to accept all of these feelings without judgment or shame and found that the more she could accept herself and her own struggle with having an autistic child, the more she could love and accept him as he was.

Self-compassion is about being kind, caring, and supportive of ourselves when we're struggling just as we would take care of a good friend. If you're like most of us, you are a much better friend to others than to yourself. As Neff says, "If you treated your friends the way you treat yourself, you would have no friends."

Research shows that 80 percent of us are more compassionate to others than to ourselves. People who practice self-compassion enjoy myriad health benefits, including reacting to stress with lower levels of stress hormones and having less anxiety and depression. As Neff points out, increased self-compassion also leads to reduced negative mind states such as shame, suicidal ideation, negative body image, and disordered eating. Likewise, self-compassion is related to enhanced immune function, life satisfaction, happiness, gratitude, self-confidence, and body appreciation.

Self-compassion can also be a powerful source of strength, coping, and resilience. One study of divorced couples, for example, found that the most reliable indicator of how they were doing one year post-divorce was whether they were a good friend to themselves. Similarly, for veterans just back from combat, self-compassion was more predictive of post-traumatic stress disorder (PTSD) than the level of combat exposure. *So it's not what happens to us but how we treat ourselves when times are tough. It comes down to whether we are most often our own inner enemy or ally.*

Here's a quick illustration of what being kind to yourself could look like in your daily life. Let's say you have had a very long day at work and finally make it home exhausted at around 8 p.m. Being kind to yourself that evening would entail not getting back on your email but taking the rest of the evening off, and relaxing in one of your favorite ways.

....

Perfection doesn't make you feel perfect. It makes you feel inadequate.

—MARIA SHRIVER

So why isn't self-compassion valued in our culture? And why is it so hard for us to be our own best friend? You may be thinking that it's more honest and honorable to be self-critical. Perhaps you see self-compassion as indulgent, lazy, selfish, self-centered, or weak.

What other misgivings do you have about self-compassion? Although we all need to have a realistic sense of our strengths and weaknesses, that's not the same as being hard on ourselves. Think of self-compassion as cultivating an inner strength that will help us every day. We become more resilient by learning to rely on ourselves for encouragement and support, just as we rely on good friends in times of grief and consolation as well as celebration.

For those of you who are curious about how self-compassionate you are, Neff developed a twenty-six-item Self-Compassion Scale to measure self-compassion. Good news: Thinking that a shorter version might be useful given time constraints, Neff and her team developed one with just twelve questions called the Self-Compassion Scale—Short Form:

SELF-COMPASSION SCALE—SHORT FORM

1. When I fail at something important to me, I become consumed by feelings of inadequacy.

2. I try to be understanding and patient toward those aspects of my personality I don't like.

3. When something painful happens, I try to take a balanced view of the situation.

4. When I'm feeling down, I tend to feel like most other people are probably happier than I am.

5. I try to see my failings as part of the human condition.

6. When I'm going through a very hard time, I give myself the caring and tenderness I need.

7. When something upsets me, I try to keep my emotions in balance.

8. When I fail at something that's important to me, I tend to feel alone in my failure.

9. When I'm feeling down, I tend to obsess and fixate on everything that's wrong.

10. When I feel inadequate in some way, I try to remind myself that feelings of inadequacy are shared by most people.

11. I'm disapproving and judgmental about my own flaws and inadequacies.

12. I'm intolerant and impatient toward those aspects of my personality I don't like.

~~~~~~

You may be wondering what the difference is between self-compassion and self-esteem. Self-esteem is defined as the positive and negative evaluations we hold about ourselves, or how we feel about ourselves. Self-compassion, on the other hand, has all of the benefits of self-esteem without the drawbacks because it excludes self-criticism, and it's not linked to social comparison the way self-esteem is. You may be aware that psychologists extolled the benefits of self-esteem until recent research linked high self-esteem with narcissism, unstable self-worth, and distorted self-perception. As Neff describes it, our self-esteem "bounces up and down like a ping-pong ball based on our latest success or failure. Self-compassion is there for us when we succeed, but it steps in precisely when self-esteem deserts us, and that's when we fail, or are humiliated in some way, then it's there to catch us."

Self-compassion is linked with fewer social comparisons and less contingent self-worth. Making fewer social comparisons can come in handy especially when glimpsing into others' worlds on social media or the Internet, which increasingly compounds the negative effects of social comparisons. We'll be discussing more on social media later.

....

Between the stimulus and the response there is a space,
and in this space lies our power and our freedom.
—USUALLY ATTRIBUTED TO VIKTOR FRANKL

Formal and Informal Practices

We can be mindful of all and any aspects of our life experiences, including sensations in our bodies, feeling, thinking, seeing, smelling, hearing, touching, and tasting. Ideally, Presence would permeate as many of our moments as possible—a tall order for sure—but the point is that Presence or mindful awareness can become more and more a way of life, a baseline way of being. Research reveals that Presence is a learnable skill. Remember, it's a practice, after all.

There are two complementary ways to realize this transformative potential of being present or mindful: formal and informal. Formal practices have a specified form, including structure and duration. Examples include mindful awareness practices such as mindfulness meditation, yoga, tai chi, or qigong. Informal practices have no specified form, but are no less important than formal practices. Examples include feeling the rain on your face, being fully present for a conversation with a friend, or catching the sunset and paying attention to nature's light show. The informal practices are important in realizing the full transformative potential of Presence in our daily lives.

Tandy and her partner found themselves in a highly stressful situation when they had to evacuate their home because of a California wildfire. She recalls packing essentials in the dark with no electricity and "being so mindful with my stuff, my toothbrush, everything . . . I had to know where things were, and what I had packed, as we prepared to flee and move not only ourselves, but our new rescue dog, Soba Noodle, and two cats, Ivy and Charlie, to the evacuation space." Tandy described the experience like a reset for her as she was so mindful during the evacuation, and ever since then she frequently asks herself, "What am I doing at this moment?"

Tandy's story illustrates an informal mindfulness practice in an extreme situation. What about during a more ordinary day—what might that look like? Amanda is in her mid-thirties, a single mom of two children, working full time as a speech therapist for her local school district, volunteering at school, and being the primary caregiver for her mother, who lives an hour away. She feels like a hummingbird, managing so many things, and fears being motionless for too long. So when she's at work she tries to be fully present with her patients, when she's volunteering she tries to pay attention to the students and what's going on in the classroom, and she makes a special effort while driving to visit her mother to feel her hands on the steering wheel, being as present as she can during that one hour.

There's one more thing I'd like to share about Amanda. She feels guilty for not having a meditation practice because she knows it would be good for her, but for now she tries as best as she can to set her intention to be present for as many moments as possible. Amanda is not alone in feeling guilty. Many of the women whom I interviewed expressed feeling guilty for not having a regular, formal meditation practice. Amanda describes it this way: "There's so much science that says I should meditate that it quickly becomes another source of guilt and it feels bad not to meditate, just as I feel guilty about not working out." One more source of guilt is the last thing any of us needs. I assured Amanda that her informal ways of practicing mindfulness in her daily activities, such as feeling her hands on the steering wheel while driving, all support and strengthen a state of Presence. No need to feel guilty. We can celebrate even one breath.

The informal is as important as the formal, so please don't despair if you don't have a formal mindfulness practice and aren't inclined to start one right now. If you do have a formal practice, then perhaps you can infuse as many moments as possible with Presence outside of your formal practice time. Formal and informal practices go hand in hand and support each other.

Kelly is thirty-nine, tall, poised, and eager to talk, perhaps because of her relatively solitary workdays as a psychotherapist. She walks into my office with her athletic stride (I later learned she played college basketball), both confident and cheerful. Kelly is the main breadwinner for her bicultural and bilingual household. Her career consists of cobbling together a private psychotherapy practice, two teaching jobs, and a small business that grants continuing education credits to mental health professionals. Kelly is now eight months pregnant and finding that her resentment grows daily as her responsibilities expand with the imminent arrival of their second baby; her spouse has a simpler life, as he not only has "just one job to deal with" but returns home to fewer responsibilities than she has for their family and home. Kelly says that her mindfulness practice is what keeps her calm. It consists of taking fifteen extra minutes in bed when she first wakes up each morning to listen to a meditation tape. Other times she meditates on her own. Kelly feels the difference on those days when she doesn't take this time for herself, and she adds, "For me, more Presence means less anxiety."

Kelly also practices mindfulness informally, "slowing down by being aware of the sounds and whatever else is happening around me. That's how I've always kept myself present." When she feels present, she describes feeling "empowered." When she is fully present at work, for example, while with a patient or during breaks between patients, she feels more connected and calm.

I had the pleasure of interviewing Kelly again after the birth of her second baby. Parenthood has taught her that "things change so fast that there's no place to be but present." Kelly realized on the morning of our second interview that her six-month-old daughter can now sit up and doesn't need to be propped up on pillows; part of parenting, she says, is being present in order to "keep up with the development."

Brewer calls the brain a pleasure-seeking machine. As he explains, once we teach the brain that resting calmly in the present feels better than our habitual state of seeking, then over time the brain will actually want more mindfulness. It turns out that our levels of well-being, resilience, and impulse control can be en-

Mindfull v. Mindful

hanced. Imagine how refreshing it would be if you could replace your "monkey-mind morning" with a more peaceful start such as mindfully drinking a cup of tea, taking a walk, or some other practice that brings you an inner sense of calm.

The More Expert We Become, the Less We See

When our brains receive stimuli, they do their job by first sorting all of the stimuli that come our way, then looking for patterns, and finally constructing categories and concepts in order to make sense of the input based on our previous experiences. This information flow can be called *top-down processing*, and it often serves us very well. Imagine if we had to start anew with everything we encounter in a day—for example, if you had to learn each morning how your coffeemaker works or how to drive a car.

Research psychologist Ellen Langer explains that actively noticing differences is the key to Presence, and that it is our expertise that gets in the way. One way of understanding this is that our top-down processing means that our minds are filled with memories, stories, and experiences from childhood on, which can sometimes imprison us and get in the way of our being able to have a fresh look at something. Ironically, the more expert we become, the less we can see, because our learning from past experiences filters our perception.

Part of our eagerness to always fill in the blanks is because *our brain prefers answers over ambiguity* and we like knowing or at least thinking that we know. When we provide a story that allows the brain to protect us, it's happy and we can enjoy a chemical reward for the story regardless of its accuracy. This phenomenon explains in part why "just be present" sounds so simple and yet in practice is so hard to incorporate into our lives. Getting comfortable with uncertainty and not knowing is part of our challenge: *not knowing is OK.*

Our family's tale of the purple bag illustrates what an amazing storyteller our brain is. When Dan and I returned from a trip to San Francisco with Alex and Maddi, our then school-aged children, we couldn't locate the purple carry-on bag that we always brought with us on trips. I thought I last saw it all packed up and ready to go at our front door before our trip, Dan thought he remembered putting it in the car, and our kids thought they last saw it in our hotel room. We retraced our steps, searched our house and car, and called the hotel, but no sign of the purple bag. One day, while looking for Maddi's volleyball shoes, I found the purple bag on the floor of the closet. It turned out that the purple bag had never left our house! We were all shocked by this and most of all by the convincing stories that each one of us had created regarding the bag's whereabouts. Our brains love stories, truth aside. Stories help us try to make sense of things, and even help us socially construct a shared view of reality, as our family did with the missing purple bag.

By contrast, with *bottom-up processing* we receive and perceive input directly through our five senses: seeing, smelling, tasting, hearing, and touching. We can even feel what scientists call our sixth sense—*interoception*—or our way of feeling the sensations of the body. This is a direct way of noticing, free of filtering through prior expectations or judgments. Langer's research shows that when we create a mindful state that can be understood as bottom-up, we experience a spaciousness and an ability to see details, which in turn allow us to live more fully in the present.

....

Nothing lasts, nothing is finished, nothing is perfect.
—RICHARD POWELL

Dispelling the Myths

What are the myths about ourselves and managing our lives that still have a hold on us? When I started listening more deeply not only to my own inner voice but also to the women in my office, my interviewees, and women in my workshops, I realized that regardless of ages and stages, we all share similar challenges. *We often find ourselves trapped in stories that have withstood the test of time but not of truth.* We underestimate and downplay our abilities, skills, and worth. The myths of "I'm not good enough" and its cousin "I don't deserve it" are alive and pervasive when it comes to women appreciating themselves and giving credit where credit is due. One business consultant whom I interviewed who works extensively in Silicon Valley said she's shocked how prevalent impostor syndrome is in so many successful women who feel "less than" or incompetent.

Joy is a single mom, an occupational therapist, one of the most accomplished and capable women I know who has worked in various clinical settings while raising her two children. She's the one you can count on to host friends and family for holidays and birthdays, always managing to bring people together when no one else seems to be able to do it. Joy declined to be interviewed for this book and when I asked her why, she said, "I'm such an underachiever. Compared to what I could have done, I've missed the mark. I should be in a better place now." Sound familiar?

Although men attribute their success to "core skills," women ascribe their success to "being lucky," "working hard," and "having support from others along the way." Male students consistently overestimate their grade point average (GPA), while women underestimate, and when it comes to job hunting, women tend to not even apply for jobs if they don't meet *all* of the qualifications for the position, while men apply if they meet only 60 percent. Furthermore, upon finding jobs, nearly 60 percent of men negotiate their first salary, while less than 10 percent of women do.

Anna, age forty-eight, has two teenagers and works full time as a commercial architect and cofounder with her architect husband of a successful firm bearing his family name in Minneapolis. Anna also teaches in the local university's architecture program, sits on the city's architectural review board, and does extensive networking that constitutes the firm's biggest revenue source. By all outward accounts Anna has a successful career. At the close of our interview, Anna asked if she could add one more thing. She leaned over and whispered, "I have been a principal in our firm for over twenty years, but I have never had a paycheck." I was incredulous. She explained that their firm has always operated as a sole proprietorship under her husband's name, and she hadn't given it a second thought until our interview. She reasoned that as long as she's married, she thinks she'll be OK.

Regardless of our age, professional status, or educational background, many of us continue to view our own power and worth in the world as "less than." That's the culturally constructed story many women carry as a top-down filter that shapes not only our beliefs and behavior, but also our sense of self. Before I left Anna that day, I recommended that she at least look into the possibility of forming a corporation and drawing a salary. I'm happy to report that two months later she let me know that she now receives a salary, for the first time in her career.

There are several other myths related to "I'm not good enough," including "I'm not smart enough, efficient enough, or fast enough." Take your pick. We often think there's something wrong with us if we can't keep up or that we aren't acceptable the way we are. This is how the story we've constructed from our social experiences shapes our views of ourselves. I asked the women whom I interviewed, regardless of age, what advice they would have for women in earlier stages of life. Their advice consistently reflected the myths we may hold: "Don't be afraid to shed your mask," "You are enough," and "Be who you are."

Another myth is that self-care is selfish. I use the term *self-care* to include self-compassion. Women often put others first, from family to friends to work, and believe that not to do so is selfish, self-centered, or self-important. Both societal and cultural expectations as well as expectations from family, friends, and those we impose on ourselves account for this.

Take a few moments now to let your most familiar myths come to mind. For me, *"I can do it all"* is a hefty one, and the one I have struggled with the most. It haunts me daily. Until I started interviewing women for this book, I thought that my generation owned this myth; surely the generations of women who have come after me, now in their twenties through their fifties, aren't trying to do it all anymore. I was wrong. It continues to be challenging for most of us to give ourselves permission to stop trying to do it all—and all so well.

The ongoing conversation we may have with ourselves around the "I can do it all" myth includes *"I'll get caught up this weekend," "I'll have more time when this project is over, when I change jobs, when I finish my training, when Dad moves into assisted living, when both kids leave for college* (fill in the blank)." What happens when those magical future points in time become our present moments?

Think about a time in your life when you thought you would enjoy more time. Did that come to pass? I hope it did, but most often it doesn't work out that way, as there's usually never enough time, much less more time. A few months after she had retired as a school administrator, my mother-in-law, Sue, said to me, "You will actually feel you have less time as you move through your life." I didn't believe her then, as I was still deep in the trenches with young children and working full time; I couldn't imagine a busier or more complicated life. I was wrong.

Once we move away from these destructive, nonproductive, but powerful myths—these inaccurate stories—we can begin to stop feeling "less than" when our days or weeks don't feel balanced. How could they be balanced? *After all, life is messy.* The takeaway: *Expect and accept messiness.* Our days are shaped by planned commitments plus the unexpected. Of course, you can't work out at the gym, drop your child off at school, get to the office by 8 a.m., meet the plumber at your apartment, catch your daughter's afternoon soccer game, pick up your car at the repair shop, visit your aunt who is in the hospital, and cook a nutritious, delicious dinner, all in the same day— or even in the same week or three weeks. But some version of this is exactly what many of us are trying to do, day after day.

The facts change, but the mythical parade of daily demands and expectations, from ourselves and others, persists. There is no one simple answer or fix, and systemic social change is also critical in addressing these messages and myths. However, cultivating our capacity to be present, to see as clearly as we can, means moving one step further away from the magnetic pulls of these myths and one step closer to more well-being.

Growing Access to Our Most Flexible Selves

Neuroscientist Amishi Jha grew up in India watching her parents practice meditation daily, to which she said no thanks; her resistance softened, however, when she observed her mother's resilience after her father's passing. Jha became curious about the science underlying meditation and now spends her life researching the benefits of meditation, primarily with groups of first responders, students, medical professionals, and the military. She practices daily and mentioned that she was about to start her meditation recently when she opted for what she calls "mom meditation" and phoned her mom in India, who had recently contracted dengue fever. Jha explained that she was fully present for the call: "It's the practice. A way of life."

As director of her science lab, mom, wife, friend, daughter, sister, and lecturer, Jha understands well the demands facing women: "Part of the nature of what happens due to the demands upon us is that we are in a state of depletion of our cognitive resources which translates to, for example, snapping at our kids. We don't want to do that; we know that is not what they need right now but we just want them to put their shoes on and leave the house for school. *We know better* but *we can't do better.* Retail therapy, vacations, exercise—nothing is giving us the access to do better."

For Jha, it's about "not letting my state of mind catch me off-guard," so she recalibrates thanks to her mindfulness practice, which includes informal practices in her everyday life, such as mom meditation and taking quiet time. In Jha's view, women value mindfulness as their lifeline. For each of us, a mindfulness practice can build resilience, by growing access to our own resources, so that it's available when we most need it.

I think that being here is it, and that ten thousand times a day you can slow a little and throw one savoring glimpse at the miracle of being around. I think that ultimately the test of even very rigorous practice over long years is actually to invest all of the non-practice moments with the presence. I think the presence is it.

—JOHN O'DONOHUE

You Can Do This

For purposes of a mini-experiment, let's pretend that your mind wandered just now; perhaps you're feeling angry about something, worried about a project, or distracted by a push notification. Pick any one of the things in the following list, all of which have been used successfully by real people, and take just one minute, or less, any place, any time. We are starting slowly and simply. As with all of the exercises in this book, the more time you can spare, the better, but even a few seconds is a solid start. Remember, just pick one!

1. THIS MOMENT. THIS BREATH. Whether you are sitting or standing right now, start by focusing your attention on the sensation of the breath as the air moves in and out of your nostrils. When breathing in, sense the in breath; when breathing out, sense the out breath. Focus on the breath for a minute, or as long as your time allows right now.

2. A SINGLE, VISUAL OBJECT. Pick one thing to focus on: the morning light through the window, a tree, a shadow. Just savor it.

3. A SINGLE ACTIVITY. Select something you do daily, such as putting on your shoes or walking out your front door. Let it fill up your entire awareness; be fully present for it.

4. THANK-YOU EMAIL. Send one thank-you email to someone who made your life a little bit better.

5. DIGITAL BREAK. Go offline, perhaps placing your phone in a drawer or making your screen dark, for just a few seconds. Repeat when you can.

6. OBSERVE. Pick something ordinary that you wouldn't usually spend time looking at and observe it deeply: perhaps an apple, a leaf, a piece of pottery. Notice everything you can about it. As Yogi Berra once said, "You can observe a lot by just watching."

Here's an example of the power of just one breath. Guadalupe, in her late forties, is a single mom with a ten-year-old daughter, Juana. Guadalupe works long, unpredictable hours as an administrative assistant at a clothing manufacturer. She went back to work when Juana was six weeks old in order to meet her monthly expenses, including rent for their apartment, which is located in the best school district in her community. For a few years, promptly upon returning home each evening after work, Guadalupe would rush through her front door, set her handbag down, and Juana would rush to her "like she was Santa Claus." About a year ago, Guadalupe noticed that Juana was always busy and barely looked up when she came home, which frustrated and saddened Guadalupe. Becoming aware that Juana had entered a new stage in her life, Guadalupe now takes one deep breath as she opens her front door upon returning from work, calmly enters her house, changes her clothes, and then sets out to see Juana. Just a few seconds of Presence, one breath, can make a huge difference in our relationships and in our larger lives. Breathing in mindfully brings the mind back home to the body in just two or three seconds. It's a quick way to begin to release whatever mental activity has a hold on you. We can feel free within a few seconds. Lucky Juana!

Federal judge Cate Furay exemplifies Presence in the workplace. When I asked what being present means to her, she replied: "Much of my job is being present. It requires not multitasking." Judge Furay has three Post-its facing her when she is in session: *Don't Say It, Be Patient,* and *Be Kind.* They serve as a buffer at times such as when she would otherwise jump in to help a struggling counsel before her or react to something in a manner that she would regret later. Judge Furay recognizes that she needs to be aware of everything that's going on in her courtroom, and as soon as she notices that she's distracted, she re-centers herself by standing up. She announces to her courtroom at the beginning of most sessions that she may occasionally stand, and she also wears a watch that reminds her to take a moment and breathe. Months after our interview, I was happy to hear from Judge Furay that she may even add a sign to her bench which says: *Be Present!*

Like Guadalupe's taking a breath to give herself the buffer she needs to bring her most resilient self forth before she connects after work with Juana, Judge Furay has Post-its and her habit of standing when she becomes aware that she is distracted. I hope that these two examples of Presence in everyday home and work life encourage you to consider how you might be able to incorporate more mindful moments into your day.

Good Stress

Research shows that women have higher stress levels than men, which may challenge our physiological and psychological well-being. Take a quick pause right now to consider which of these two statements best describes how you feel about stress:

A. Stress is harmful and should be reduced, managed, or avoided; or

B. Stress is helpful and should be embraced, utilized, and welcomed.

If you selected the first statement, you are not alone. Less than ten years ago, many psychologists, doctors, and scientists crusaded against stress. Health psychologist Kelly McGonigal pointed out in *The Upside of Stress* that she held steadfast to the message that "stress is toxic" for years.

What changed McGonigal's mind about stress? A 1998 study asked thirty thousand people in the United States how much stress they had experienced in the past year, and whether they believed stress is harmful to their health. Eight years later, public records were reviewed to find out who among the thirty thousand had died. As you might guess, high levels of stress correlated with a 43 percent greater risk of dying. What you might be surprised to learn, however, and what caught McGonigal's attention, was the finding that the increased risk applied only to people *who believed that stress was also harming their health. Those who reported high stress levels but didn't view their stress as harmful were not more likely to die.* And in fact, they had the lowest risk of death in the study, even lower than those who reported experiencing low stress. How amazing and surprising is that?

Whenever anything meaningful is at stake, the physiological

arousal of stress naturally occurs. Stress in this way can be an inherent part of our engaged lives, and there's no way around that. *A meaningful life is a stressful life.* Raising children, managing aging parents, covering college tuition, working hard to heal our planet, or meeting demanding work deadlines can bring high levels of stress, but this doesn't automatically mean bad stress. It may just be evidence of a full life.

So stress may actually be good for us. The key is not to get rid of stress, but to change how we relate to it. McGonigal explains it this way: "When we think our life should be less stressful, feeling stressed can be seen as a sign that you are inadequate: If you were strong enough, smart enough, or good enough, then you wouldn't be stressed. Stress becomes a sign of personal failure rather than evidence that you are human." Not surprisingly, we are more likely to feel overwhelmed and hopeless when we're in this mindset. This underscores why our relationship to stress is so important.

Sometimes experiences are so threatening that they activate our fight, flee, freeze, and even faint response, what psychologist Carol Dweck, author of *Mindset*, calls a "threat reaction" (as in feeling anxious, fearful, uncertain, like "I can't do this"). Staying in a threat state for long periods of time can negatively impact our health, even though the initial stressor itself was not harmful. However, there are situations where a threat response is appropriate; situations involving domestic or intimate partner violence create chronic toxic stress and therefore activate threat responses in the individuals experiencing it. On the other hand, what Dweck calls a "challenge response" (hopeful, excited, confident, "I can do this") profoundly changes how demanding situations impact our lives.

Certain groups experience chronically elevated stress levels as a result of prejudices, discriminations, and marginalization they face on the basis of their identities. Social scientists use what's called *minority stress theory* to study why and how minority individuals experience poorer mental and physical health than their counterparts in majority groups. This theory holds true for racial and ethnic, as well as gender and sexual minorities. Some studies have also taken into account intersectionality and illustrated its prevalence across groups. One study, for example, illustrated the relationship between minority stress and elevated levels of anxiety and depression in LGBTQ+ individuals.

The Motherhood Penalty and the Fatherhood Bonus

Women with children struggle to adapt their careers to the demands of child-rearing and are often viewed differently from their male counterparts because they don't fit the mold of the leaders— primarily men—who have preceded them. We are often expected to show our unwavering devotion and allegiance to both work and our children, and are held accountable in ways that men are not. Have you ever left your office early to attend your daughter's soccer game or some other event? Or gone to work late because your son's preschool had a holiday celebration that morning? Those of you who are parents may even have received negative feedback about your choices, as I have, including that you are not taking your work seriously enough. On the other hand, when a male colleague leaves work early to attend his child's sporting event, you may have heard that he's a great dad—with no negative reflection upon his work.

Canada-based Jacqueline Carter and Denmark-based Rasmus Hougaard often work together as business partners of Potential

Project, a global provider of leadership and organizational effectiveness solutions based on training the mind. By all appearances, Jacqueline and Rasmus lead very similar lives at work and at home. Both have twenty years of experience working with international organizations; both have a quick smile, gentle spirit, and clear mind that draws you in from the first moment you meet them; both also have twins with their respective spouses. I think that they even look alike. It's no surprise that they're so successful in rolling out mindfulness training programs for corporations around the globe, including Accenture, Cisco, Lego, Marriott, IKEA, and Microsoft, to name a few.

When I asked Jacqueline about the motherhood penalty, she gave this example: When Rasmus leads a training program and opens with a story about his kids, the feedback from the audience is glowing, along the lines of, "What an amazing man, so successful, yet kind." When Jacqueline opens with the exact same content and mentions her kids, the feedback often reflects less support and respect. She noted, "As an experienced presenter, you know whether you have captured the audience or not . . . and for me, as a woman, mentioning that I am a parent is a potential detractor as it makes me appear less professional, whereas for Rasmus, it is a bonus because it makes him seem more human."

Business leaders espouse "family-friendly" values, but in a recent survey, 40 percent stated that the best workers "are those without a lot of personal commitments," reflecting the stringent, consuming attitudes of the high-intensity workplace. Approximately two thirds of male senior managers in the United States have children, compared to just one third of female senior managers. Since familial responsibilities are typically associated with women, women are less likely to meet expectations for the "best worker."

Generally, employers have been seen rewarding fathers more than mothers, something academics call the "motherhood penalty" and the "fatherhood bonus," whereby fathers get "extra credit" while mothers are perceived as less devoted because they have children.

So long as caregiving for children and elders is viewed as a woman's problem, companies, as well as our larger society, avoid changing our culture in ways that would benefit both women and men. For example, providing paternity or family leave sends a message that family life is a priority for all. Parents dropping their children off at school, taking time off when they're ill, attending school events, and going on family vacations isn't slacking; it's equally important work.

The *worry work* or *mental load* continues to fall mostly on Mom's shoulders to anticipate and organize what the kids need. Dad is happy to take the kids to the dentist, but it's usually Mom who is masterminding the schedule. Studies of heterosexual couples confirm that mothers draft the to-do lists while fathers pick and choose among items, while several studies have shown that lesbian and gay couples are generally more egalitarian in their division of labor. Research on other groups in the LGBTQ+ community is limited, but one study suggests that female partners of transgender men carry the brunt of the housework and emotional work. Research has also found that mothers' paid work hours increase when children's activities decrease, while fathers' paid hours are not affected by how much their children do.

Permeating all of this, is our unconscious, gendered assumptions about what makes a good leader. Respondents in one study said *someone named Eric who offered new ideas was a natural leader, while someone named Erica who offered the same ideas was not.* Men are seen as having leadership qualities like gravitas, while women are seen as having supportive-role qualities like dependability.

I want to acknowledge here that parenting responsibilities do not apply to all women, nor is parenting the only source of work-life challenges for women. Although cultural messages and expectations may be that women are "supposed to have children" or "want children," some of us don't, for whatever reason, by choice or not. Cecilia decided early in her life to not have children. About her decision, Cecilia explained with exasperation, "No one can believe it. I'm Asian. It's not just relatives, but cabdrivers, and even my own female physician." Cecilia hopes that since she is now in her forties, the disbelief and questions will soon stop.

Most, if not all of us, may hold gendered assumptions. When Anne-Marie Slaughter first became the dean at Princeton in 2002, she attempted to change the norms by deliberately talking about her children; she also ended faculty meetings at 6 p.m., mentioning that she was going home for dinner with her family. After a few months of this, several female assistant professors showed up in her office agitated. "You *have* to stop talking about your kids," one said. "You are not showing the gravitas that people expect from a dean, which is particularly damaging, precisely because you are the first woman dean of the school." Slaughter found it interesting that gravitas and parenthood don't seem to go together, and told the professors that she was doing it deliberately and would continue.

Is Mindfulness the Same as Meditation?

....

One does not practice meditation to become a great meditator. We meditate to wake up and live, to become skilled at the art of living.

—ELIZABETH LESSER

Let's turn next to the connection between mindfulness and meditation. As I'm using the terms *Presence*, *mindfulness*, and *mindful awareness* synonymously as we've discussed, you may wonder if *meditation* is another synonym. The answer is, it depends on who is using the terms. There's plenty of confusion. It may help to think of meditation as the larger concept, the mental training that can facilitate our being in a state of mindfulness, mindful awareness, or Presence more often. As psychologist Daniel Goleman and neuroscientist Richard Davidson point out in their book *Altered Traits*, even some scientists use the term *mindfulness* "as a stand-in for any and all kinds of meditation. And in popular usage, mindfulness can refer to meditation in general, despite the fact that mindfulness is but one of a variety of methods."

The word *meditation* is a catch-all term for the many ways we can train the mind, just as *sports* or *exercise* refers to a wide range of different athletic activities, with each type providing its own unique benefits. Although certain mindfulness meditation practices, such as breathing exercises, are associated with relaxation or calm states, meditation is active mental training, and many mindfulness practices can leave us feeling invigorated. Studies comparing mindfulness practices to relaxation training show that they have different effects. So meditation is not necessarily a relaxing activity in and of itself, although it can be.

You may be brand new to meditation or in the "just thinking about it" phase but unclear on what exactly it can do for you. If you take just thirty seconds right now, which is plenty of time for this little experiment, and sit comfortably while focusing on your breath, you will experience firsthand how challenging it can be to train your attention. Our minds are aptly called "monkey minds" by meditation teachers, as they constantly drift to plans, regrets, fantasies, and things other than the object of our intended focus. Striving to calm our mind down only seems to make it worse, but eventually with meditation practice our minds do calm down, and more space arises for more subtle things to enter.

As we spend more time in the present, our intuition becomes more available to us, we may begin to see things more clearly, and some may experience what they describe as an "expansiveness." Meditation isn't just for the times when we're stressed, overwhelmed, or facing illness. And it's not just for working moms, career women, or yoga practitioners. It's for everyone, across the diversity of humanity and in a wide variety of settings, including our homes, schools, hospitals, parks, prisons, military bases, and homeless shelters.

What's Keeping Us from Meditating?

For some, meditation may still suffer from what news anchor Dan Harris in his book *10% Happier* calls its "PR problem," which dates back to the 1960s and 1970s, when meditation was popularized in the United States and associated with robed gurus and hippies. Catchphrases such as *just breathe, simply let go,* and *smile with your heart* may not resonate with many in our hard-driving, no-nonsense world.

However, much has changed over the past fifteen years and with increased research supporting its benefits, there is a growing interest in working out with our minds. That's what meditation is: training the mind. One morning, a friend of mine who doesn't meditate but is curious asked me: "Do you know what the hardest part about meditation is?" Before I could say anything, she answered: "It's doing it." I had to agree with her. Finding time in the day to meditate can be challenging for all of us. We have complex lives, with work, medical challenges, families, aging parents, hobbies, bills, friends, emergencies, pets, travel, calls, emails . . . being a human is very demanding.

Recently I convinced myself (temporarily) that on that particular day I couldn't take time to meditate—after all, it was our daughter Maddi's twenty-third birthday, we had a houseguest, I had meetings all afternoon, I was leaving town the next day . . . you get the picture. What I remind myself on such days—when I'm being mindful—are the words of mindfulness teacher Trudy Goodman: "To maintain your meditation practice, you need to be ruthless. Not to meditate is stealing from ourselves." I often think of Trudy's words because they underscore the challenge we all face. We must intentionally not only set aside the meditation time but protect it so that it is actually available to us.

The most common reasons that keep us from meditating are listed in the following table. I realize that I'm providing these at the risk of offering some of you more reasons not to meditate! See if any of them ring true for you.

OVERCOMING WHAT'S KEEPING US FROM MEDITATING

The Reason	The Workaround
I have no time to meditate.	This may be the number one excuse among people who want to meditate but never get around to doing it. If you are so inclined, give it a try for one week. Even one, two, or three minutes of meditation a day can make a difference. It's important to meet yourself where you are. On your terms. When you are ready. All of the compelling science and convincing stories will not do as much as your own experience in showing you what difference meditating may make in your life. As my aunt Pearl would say, "The proof is in the pudding."
I'll lose my edge. I'll become passive and weak.	These are myths and, in fact, the opposite is true. Consider that you will develop new strengths: better executive functioning and more focus, which mean greater efficiency.
I don't deserve it.	For those of you who think meditation is selfish, self-indulgent, and that you don't deserve it, consider the words of mindfulness teacher Sharon Salzberg: "The first thing you need to be able to say to yourself is: 'I'm worth ten minutes a day.'"
I'm too stressed to meditate right now.	When we're most stressed, meditation can be very helpful, so it can be an especially important time to meditate. However, if you're just starting a practice, it can be best—if you have the option—to do so when you are not in a crisis.

I can't sit still.	You could start with a one-minute sitting meditation and build from there. If it's the sitting you don't like, try one of the many other practices, such as qigong, yoga, Pilates, or even walking meditation.
I'm terrible at it.	As Jon Kabat-Zinn says: "If you're doing it, you're doing it right." There is no wrong way and no need to judge.
My mind is too busy.	We all have "monkey minds" with constant thought loops. Remember that being present means a clear mind, not an empty mind.
My mind is a Pandora's box.	You may fear what you may find when you become still. Although something fearful may arise, it was not created by the meditation, and if it does exist it may be beneficial to become aware of it and decide whether to address it.
I'm in my mind enough.	Meditation actually breaks the momentum of our infinite thought loops and brings us out of our thoughts and more in touch with our senses.
I tried meditation, and although it may work for you, it doesn't work for me.	Just as it takes time to figure out our preferred physical workouts, it takes time to find the mindfulness practices that work best for each one of us.
Terrible things still kept happening in my life, so what's the point?	Frustrations and misfortunes will neither stop nor decline, but our relationship to such situations will change as we build resiliency and the confidence that we can deal with whatever comes our way.

You may want to start your mindfulness practice before you feel you really need it, but that's not how it usually works. Many of us don't get serious about meditation until a crisis is upon us. Ruchika Sikri was just three months into her new job at Google when a family member had a medical emergency. Ruchika felt that she had "no hard hat" and "no ground beneath her," so she began practicing yoga and started to meditate. To this day, she continues her practices.

Some of us may have had a practice on and off for several years. As one of my interviewees put it, she was "just fooling with it," but recognized that meditating daily "would definitely be beneficial." Getting out of a daily practice routine can make it hard to resume, but after a few stops and starts, many have been able to sustain a practice. Kimberly is forty-nine, the picture of health, and looks so confident, perhaps because I know she's the cofounder of a successful start-up company. She begins our interview by telling me that about three months ago, she received a diagnosis of stomach cancer, and the one thing that is getting her through is her meditation practice of five years. She explains that it took her a long time to establish a regular practice. Years earlier when she faced a health challenge, she received a meditation CD from a friend, practiced for one year and then stopped.

Five years later, while experiencing chronic health problems that neither her doctors nor other health professionals could assist with, Kimberly pulled out the meditation CD and listened to it. Kimberly meditated regularly for the next three years and was finally experiencing relief from some of her health challenges. When she received her diagnosis of cancer, she became what she calls "a caretaker for myself," and feels grateful that she already had her meditation practice securely in place. Defying all medical expectations, the markers for Kimberly's cancer are declining steadily each day, and she says that she is happier than ever before because she is shedding layers of what others think of her and is sure that she can tackle whatever comes her way.

When Trudy Goodman broke her spine a few months ago, at a time when she also had poison oak all over her body, she was disappointed that she couldn't do all the things she had planned for the near future. She said that her meditation practice saved her, as she wasn't exacerbating her situation with more suffering from her own frustration, catastrophizing, and disappointment. Trudy was able to spare herself the suffering of "piling on," which is what many of us tend to do in times of challenge. Suffering can be caused by our resisting what is. Trudy's story provides a beautiful example of the power of Presence in our daily lives. While we cannot control the pain of life's events, we do have control over how we choose to respond to events and can minimize our suffering by accepting them as they already are, rather than resisting them.

Different Types of Meditation Practices

As I've mentioned, there are many different types of meditation practices and as with physical training, each type gives rise to its own unique and most likely outcome. For example, one type is mindfulness meditation, which generally includes the cultivation of (a) *focused attention*, (b) *open monitoring* (a spacious awareness of whatever comes to mind), and, for some researchers, (c) *compassion* or *lovingkindness* meditation. In the first type, focused attention meditation, which is usually the starting point for a beginning meditator, we aim to center the mind in the present moment by focusing on a chosen single object or stimulus, such as our breath. To maintain this focus, we need to constantly monitor our concentration on the chosen object to avoid mind-wandering. As soon as we become aware of a distraction, as we notice our attention is no longer on the designated object or activity, we redirect our attention back to the object of our focus. Focused attention training can help us begin to have awareness and management over our attention, strengthening our capacity to sustain our attention and redirect it when it wanders, building the foundation for fully inhabiting the present moment.

After we become familiar with focused attention meditation and can take part in the effort to sustain our attentional focus for a considerable amount of time (let's say fifteen or twenty minutes for a beginner and more for longtime practitioners), we may choose to try a second kind of meditation called open monitoring meditation, which does not involve any object or event as the focus. The practice here involves the monitoring of awareness itself; that is, we remain open and attentive to whatever experience may arise, without selecting, judging, clinging to, or focusing on any particular object or event. We observe and note phenomena as they come and go, keeping our attention flexible; it's a spacious awareness of whatever comes to mind. Some teachers recommend naming what comes to your attention, such as *sound*, *feeling*, or *sensation*, and then letting it go. The key is that our awareness is open to whatever arises but doesn't get carried away or overtaken by any one thing. We are simply resting in awareness.

We can practice open monitoring informally by taking a moment here and there throughout our day to notice and observe what thoughts, feelings, or sensations are arising for us—perhaps by setting such an intention before a meeting or difficult conversation. Similarly, we can set our intention to take in smells, sights, and sensations during a walk, such as feeling the wind on our face. Poet Diane Ackerman does what she calls a "walkabout" each morning in her garden and pays attention to shadows and smells. We can be present for any of our everyday tasks, and the more moments we can completely inhabit the present, the calmer we will feel. Remember, for as many moments as you can be present, that will be enough for right now. Try it out for yourself. Also, please don't forget to treasure the informal practices as much as the formal; both are beneficial. Most important, please don't be hard on yourself if you don't have a regular, formal practice at all right now.

In a third type of mindfulness meditation, compassion or lovingkindness meditation, we extend feelings of love and compassion to others and ourselves, incorporating elements of both focused attention and open monitoring. Practitioners focus on developing love and compassion, usually first for ourselves (although this can be challenging for some, in which case, starting with a loved one or perhaps a pet may work well) and then gradually extending this love to others, from family and friends to strangers and ultimately to individuals with whom we are experiencing some challenge or difficulty.

Lovingkindness meditation has been associated with an increase in positive emotions, activation of empathy, an increase in prosocial behavior, and a reduction in self-criticism, among other benefits. Research has also shown that meditation incorporating all three types of mindfulness meditation—focused attention, open monitoring, and lovingkindness—cultivates well-being in those who practice it.

You may be wondering, "How does lovingkindness meditation relate to the other two types of meditation we have been discussing?" Here's one way to think about it: Let's say you are doing an open monitoring practice, that is, setting your intention to pay attention to whatever arises: sounds, smells, the sensation of the air on your face. Invariably your mind will wander, and quite predictably you may find your thoughts turning to something like the argument you had last night with your roommate. Rather than getting upset with yourself, thinking that you can't even do a simple practice and stay on task, reframe your response by being kind to yourself in those split seconds, and recall that mind-wandering is ingrained in all of us. One of the most amazing things about a meditation practice is that the very instant you realize that you are not paying attention, you are already back on task. How many other things in our lives have such a quick fix?

We have discussed just three types of meditation practice here, but there are many others. Also in one sitting, or meditation session, you could choose to practice all three kinds. You could, for example, begin with focused attention on your breath and then move to open monitoring, and then to lovingkindness. No matter what type of meditation you choose to practice, certain qualities are likely to arise, unique to each type, such as a stable and clear mind, emotional balance, and a sense of love and compassion. One student put it this way: "I always thought it was about what happens during the meditation, but that's not it. It's what happens out in my life." Similarly, mindfulness leader Sharon Salzberg reminds us, "We don't meditate to get better at meditating. We meditate to get better at life."

The Benefits of Mindfulness

Let's turn now to the major health benefits of mindfulness, including reducing stress, strengthening our attention, and slowing the aging process.

REDUCES STRESS AND ANXIETY

Anxiety and stress have sometimes been correlated with an active amygdala in the limbic area of the brain, which communicates with both the survival-oriented brain stem below it and the reasoning, story-creating cortex above it. The amygdala is our brain's radar for threat, and it plays a dual role of directing our attention and shaping our intense emotional reactions. *A chronically activated amygdala becomes a larger amygdala.* When we are upset, we become distracted as we review over and over in our minds whatever is making us anxious. This preoccupation is an example of unintentional mindwandering, which is stressful in and of itself and reduces our ability to pay attention. Take a moment now to identify that one thing that has such a hold on you that you find yourself thinking about it over and over again. It may be the last thing you think of at night and the first thing you think of each morning. And if you are like most of us, before this most current issue, there was something else, just as after this issue passes there will be another one.

What if there were a way to break this exhausting pattern and get a message to our amygdala? Good news: Mindfulness calms the amygdala, making it less reactive, thereby decreasing its size and reducing our anxiety and stress. By regulating the amygdala more effectively, the prefrontal cortex can diminish the activity and size of the amygdala over time. In this way, mindfulness practices that stimulate the growth of the regulatory prefrontal region may be how these mind trainings alter the structure of the brain and cultivate more emotional stability.

STRENGTHENS ATTENTION

With focused attention training, the brain is repeatedly engaged in a way that stabilizes attention, enabling the individual to select and maintain the focus of attention, notice when attention has wandered, redirect attention to the intended focus, and ultimately become less distractible. With open monitoring practice, we learn to distinguish the *experience of being aware* from *what it is that we are aware of.* In other words, we learn to see how mental activities like thoughts or feelings are simply objects of awareness, not the totality of our identity or absolute reality. Various brain regions are believed to be activated and grow to facilitate this strengthened attention, including aspects of the prefrontal and anterior cingulate cortex.

ENHANCES CARDIOVASCULAR FUNCTION

Mindfulness training may improve cardiovascular functions in several ways, such as lowering cholesterol, optimizing blood pressure, and helping the brain communicate in a more balanced way with the heart. The heart and brain have two-way communication with each other, and practices that include a body scan which focuses on the interior sensations of the heart region and other bodily areas may be a key component to how these mind trainings improve physiological functioning.

HELPS TREAT EATING DISORDERS

Mindful eating involves a practice of being aware of the sensation of eating and includes distinguishing the feelings of hunger and being full. For many with challenges to healthy eating, whether restricting or overeating, many complex emotions, thoughts, body image distortions, and social issues may make the process of being hungry and eating in a healthy and balanced way difficult. Mindfulness may help by providing a way to distinguish basic physiological needs for nurturance from emotionally driven issues regarding self-acceptance and social relationships that in some cases may have become symbolically represented as images of the body.

In the brain, one's image of the size and shape of the body is distinct from being aware of the body's sensations. In the case of eating challenges, the person may be preoccupied with body image while also being less aware of the body's actual sensations. Mindfulness may help people be more in touch with bodily sensations while also empowering them to see a body image preoccupation as simply a mental activity, not absolute reality or the totality of their identity.

A recent study by research psychologist Lawrence Barsalou showed changes in brain function after mindfulness training whereby he taught the participants how to de-center—that is, to observe their mind's activities and become aware that these are just activities of the mind (that is, thoughts, emotions, and memories). This training allowed them to choose healthy over unhealthy foods. We don't know the long-term effect of this intervention, but this finding along with other research provides empirical reasons for optimism for the power of mindfulness training in addressing eating disorders.

BUILDS EMPATHY AND COMPASSION

With Presence, we become aware of suffering both within ourselves and in our larger world. Empathy can be defined as having at least these five facets:

1. Emotional resonance—feeling the feelings of others

2. Perspective taking—seeing through another person's eyes

3. Cognitive empathy—understanding the mind of another person

4. Empathic joy—being happy for another's happiness and success

5. Empathic concern—caring about the welfare of another, the gateway for compassion

Empathy doesn't have an accompanying "action item," so we can feel overwhelmed or helpless if we just feel empathic without engaging our ability to be compassionate by doing something to reduce suffering. If we overidentify with the feelings of suffering, we can lose differentiation and become burnt-out.

Compassion has these three components:

1. Sensing suffering (of self or another)

2. Reflecting on how to reduce that suffering

3. Enacting behaviors to reduce suffering

In lovingkindness meditation, for example, the verbal statements are linguistic representations that likely stimulate the activity of compassion circuitry, and with repeated practice, they may strengthen these activated networks to create a more compassionate set of traits.

REDUCES INFLAMMATION AND ENHANCES IMMUNE FUNCTION

Changing the regulation of gene expression in areas of the chromosomes responsible for the inflammatory response reduces inflammation. This is called *epigenetic regulation.* By improving immune function, mindfulness practices can also help reduce the risk of infection and strengthen how we can recover from various illnesses.

Exactly how mindfulness practices alter these molecular mechanisms of health is not clear, but research suggests that mindfulness practices may be related to reduction in the stress response. When an organism is threatened, the natural protective response is to mobilize the reactive states of the brain and body to fight or flee. In the short run, this response is quite adaptive and helps us survive. Here in California, if a mountain lion is lunging at you, it's great to be able to activate this threat response to enhance your chance of survival. But sustained states of threat, also called *toxic stress*, produce increases in inflammation, accelerate aging, and lead to a higher risk of infection. There may be many ways that mindfulness practice reduces stress and inflammation, enhances immune function, and slows the aging process.

SLOWS AGING BY REPAIRING THE ENDS OF OUR CHROMOSOMES

Our telomeres are the tiny but essential ends of our chromosomes that protect our DNA, our genetic library. They are like the protective plastic tips at the ends of our shoelaces that keep them from fraying. Think of the shoelaces as our chromosomes, the structures in the nucleus or center of every cell in our body that carry our DNA. As we age, our telomeres get shorter, and when they get too short, our cells can't divide in a healthy way anymore. Our genes affect our telomeres, both their length at birth and how quickly they dwindle down. You may be surprised to learn that how we live our lives and what we do with our minds affects our telomere health as well. How? By influencing the levels of an enzyme called telomerase that works to repair, replenish, and maintain our telomeres. Optimal amounts of telomerase dictate healthy telomeres. *Presence optimizes telomerase levels.*

The way we live can speed up or slow down our cellular aging. From the foods we eat to our response to emotional challenges, several factors influence our telomeres and can prevent premature aging at the cellular level. Two scientists, Elissa Epel and Nobel Prize winner Elizabeth Blackburn, showed a relationship between stress and shorter telomeres in one of the most highly stressed caregiver groups of all: mothers who were taking care of their chronically ill children. They found that "the years of caregiving had a profound effect, grinding down the women's telomeres. The longer a mother had been looking after her sick child, the shorter her telomeres." They also found the more stressed out the mothers felt, the shorter their telomeres—and this finding held true for everyone in the study, even the control group of mothers who had healthy children at home. The high-stress mothers had half the levels of telomerase compared to the low-stress mothers, and their capacity to protect their telomeres was lower. Work stress is not related to shorter telomeres, but burnout, emotional exhaustion from work, is. This finding is consistent with what we discussed earlier about good stress; whether from work or any other part of our lives, when something meaningful is at stake, there's a physiological arousal of stress and the question is how we view the stress. Long-term exposure to stress that we view as harmful to us can have a negative impact on our health.

We can take steps to actually repair our telomeres. We want to maintain strong telomeres because our cellular health and our tissue's regenerative capacity depend on it. Mindfulness is a robust predictor of optimal amounts of telomerase, which can increase our health span (the years during which we can enjoy good health) and decrease our disease span (the months or years we may live with a disease that interferes with our quality of living).

OPTIMIZES REGULATION OF ATTENTION, EMOTION, AND MOOD

Research on the brain involving three of the types of meditation we've discussed—focused attention, open monitoring, and lovingkindness—suggests that widely separated and distinct brain areas become linked when activated. This linkage of differentiated parts of the brain can be called *neural integration*, which allows for the coordination and balance of the various functions that arise from both the distinct brain regions and the outcome of their synergistic, collaborative functions. In brief, the brain achieves optimal regulation of neural activities such as attention, emotion, mood, memory, behavior, and morality through neural integration.

A mindfulness practice creates an integrated *state* that when repeated over time becomes an integrated *trait* of well-being, as we discussed earlier. Examples of regions of the brain that have been shown to grow with mindfulness practice include the corpus callosum (which connects the right and left hemispheres), the hippocampus (which links widely separated memory regions to each other), the insula (which links the body to the cortex), and the prefrontal cortex (which links the cortex, limbic area, brain stem, body, and social world together).

Another way of assessing both functional and structural integration is by studying the *connectome*, which reveals widely distributed and differentiated areas of the brain and how they are interconnected. Connectome studies of mindfulness practitioners show increases in the "interconnectivity of the connectome" (yes, that's what the scientists call it!). These studies show that the brain becomes more integrated with mindfulness practices. Since neural integration creates mental regulation, you can begin to see how beneficial it is to cultivate more neural integration. Increased integration may be the mechanism by which mindfulness practices enhance memory, improve mood, prevent major depression relapse, and promote resilience and emotional balance in our lives.

HELPS PREVENT RELAPSE OF ADDICTIONS

Mindfulness may be involved in preventing relapse of addictions, including alcohol, drug, and tobacco dependency. Addiction involves fluctuations of dopamine levels in the brain. Meditation decreases the release of dopamine. No one knows for sure how this happens, but one recent finding is that perhaps meditation trains the mind to distinguish the brain's signals of like/prefer versus want/need/crave. Want is a gateway to need, craving, and clinging.

When we want, need, or crave something, we feel inadequate and incomplete if we don't have it. Liking, on the other hand, is a preference. If we don't have what we like at a given time, we don't feel inadequate and incomplete. Lowering the dopamine level may make it easier for us to distinguish between want and need. When we realize we don't need certain things, we feel complete, empowered, and strong.

An alteration in the dopamine-based reward circuitry in the brain may support diminished craving, which means less vulnerability to addiction. The capacity that mindfulness creates to distinguish the experience of being aware from the object of awareness may be an important, additional mental skill that would allow those with a history of addiction to feel a craving in awareness and put a space between the impulse to use a substance or engage in an activity and the actual behavior. Within that space is where choice and freedom arise. Mindfulness gives us the power to choose our behavior rather than allowing unhealthy habits or addictions to choose for us.

The following table summarizes the major health benefits of mindfulness training, which includes the strengthening of attention, open monitoring, and lovingkindness.

MAJOR HEALTH BENEFITS OF MINDFULNESS

Health Benefit	How It Works
For our mind	
Strengthens attention	Activates and strengthens attention networks, including the prefrontal and anterior cingulate cortex
Optimizes regulation	Enhances neural integration—the linkage of differentiated parts in both function and structure for optimal regulation of attention, emotion, mood, thought, memory, behaviors, and relationships
Promotes resilience and emotional balance	Supports the ability to return readily to a baseline of a calm state in the face of a challenge
Enhances memory	Promotes growth in the hippocampus and prefrontal regions, which enhances recall and working memory functions
Builds empathy and compassion	Strengthens the anterior cingulate, insula, and other regions involved in empathy and compassion, which are the neural circuits that serve as the pathways for knowing what we and others are feeling
For our physiological health	
Enhances cardiovascular function	Improves blood pressure and cholesterol levels and cultivates better communication between the brain and the heart

Reduces inflammation	Regulates an area on the genes through epigenetic control that is responsible for the inflammatory response, which means less inflammation
Prevents and fights infection	Improves our immune function, which reduces the risk of infection and strengthens our recovery from various illnesses
Slows aging	Optimizes the enzyme telomerase, which repairs and maintains our telomeres (the ends of our chromosomes), thereby increasing cellular health and decreasing cellular aging

For behavioral challenges

Reduces stress and anxiety	Lowers stress hormone (cortisol) levels and calms the amygdala by shrinking its size
Prevents major depression relapse	Enables the recognition of the signs of depression so that an early intervention can be initiated to prevent the return of depression
Helps treat eating disorders	May allow more attunement with the body, making eating more physiological than psychological
Helps prevent relapse of addictions	Increases self-awareness and decreases the release of dopamine, the neurotransmitter of the reward circuitry that is involved in addiction, which supports diminished craving and results in less vulnerability to addiction

These benefits, in turn, have profound positive effects on our executive functioning, emotional and cognitive resilience (with the growth of more integrated brain circuits), focus of attention and cognitive efficiency, and enhanced memory. These benefits help explain why so many corporate leaders are interested in rolling out mindfulness offerings for their employees. Companies such as Aetna Insurance, Ford Motor Company, Google, General Mills, Target, Eileen Fisher, and Starbucks are not only encouraging mindfulness but offering training to thousands of employees. Nike, HBO, AOL, Deutsche Bank, and Procter & Gamble provide quiet rooms for naps, prayer, and meditation, as well as meditation and yoga classes. McKinsey & Company has embraced meditation as part of its HR strategy and is developing meditation and self-analysis programs for internal use as well as use by some of its clients. Ten years ago at the Mindsight Institute, our core audience was primarily mental health professionals, and today our audience is composed of a diverse range of people from various fields, including education, business, law, government, and technology.

Similarly, programs such as Goldie Hawn's MindUP are bringing mindfulness to millions of children around the world, including in the United States, Canada, the United Kingdom, Serbia, Mexico, Hong Kong, Australia, and New Zealand. In addition, we have a wide variety of meditation apps to choose from, many of which serve as home to millions of meditators across almost every country in the world.

As the interest in mindfulness grows, and continues to be rolled out in school districts across the United States, programs need to be sensitive to the populations they are serving, including racial and ethnic minority groups. Research scientist Sará King studies the experiences of urban youth of color with yoga and meditation in school-based interventions and their impact on stress, well-being, and interpersonal relationships. She explains that interventionists in schools need to be able to relate effectively with students from diverse populations. This is important not only for mindfulness programs in schools but all across our meditation communities as mentioned earlier.

Establishing a Sustainable Mindful Awareness Practice Plan (MAPP)

It can be challenging to sustain a mindfulness practice over time. Gaps of days, weeks, months, or even years are not uncommon. It's also not uncommon to try one type of meditation and then give up, for any number of reasons, including that you feel it isn't working, or you no longer need it now that things are getting better in your life.

Looking after our minds can be like looking after our bodies; we know what we have to do, but doing it is another matter. We know it's good for us, we know why it's good for us, and it's still hard. A common roadblock to establishing a regular meditation practice is concern over the physical space for meditating. London-based Razeea Lemaignen, health and well-being consultant for GlaxoSmithKline, told me that one thing she emphasizes to the company's nearly 100,000 employees worldwide is the importance of getting past the "space barrier." She encourages meditation in the place where the stress is occurring: "no need to split meditation from stress." Many of us may think that we need to retreat to our garden or a quiet spot to meditate, but we don't always have that option. Lemaignen also discusses the importance of getting over the "perfection barrier." She explains to her students that they likely won't have an amazing "aha" moment that will fix all of their problems, but nonetheless, "a small decrease in stress translates to an enormous impact on access to your resources and provides a way to bring your best self to the situation."

Cathy is in her forties and was wearing a bright green shirt imprinted with trees on the day we met, clearly a nature lover. With her enthusiastic, firm handshake and confident presence, clipboard in hand, it was evident from the moment I met her that she can do anything she sets out to do. She has worked twelve-hour days for fifteen years to build up her landscape business. When it comes to mindfulness she says, "I feel like a failure. I'm a master time waster. I have no discipline when it comes to life balance; I'm the epitome of non-mindfulness." By the end of our interview, she was so intrigued by the prospect of having a meditation practice that she asked if we could have a check-in every two weeks, and meanwhile she would try a meditation app called Headspace.

I texted Cathy the morning of our scheduled check-in day to get a time and heard nothing. Then a text came about a day later: "How about now?" I said that could work and jokingly added that it struck me as ironic that someone who resists mindfulness is so in the moment. She said, "I don't resist. It's more neglecting," which of course can be a trap for many of us. At our check-in, Cathy said that when she sat down to meditate, she found herself making lists and thought to herself, "I'm pretty sure that making lists isn't what meditation is." As we talked more, she realized that the reason she wasn't prioritizing a practice is that she needs to get a certain number of her "life's tasks" out of her way first, from shoe repair to scheduling the plumber.

At the end of our check-in, I requested that for the next two weeks, Cathy meditate for one minute each day. She said that she actually could commit to meditating for ten minutes per day. Progress,

I thought; yay! Within four days of making her commitment, Cathy texted that she had already watched a few meditation videos. Very encouraging! Within one month of our first meeting, Cathy texted that she had been listening to several more meditations led by different teachers. I'm happy to report that now, ten months after our first meeting, I still receive regular updates from Cathy—all encouraging—as she continues her daily meditation practice.

So how do you get your own plan into place, ideally before you desperately need it? Being mindful is a way of life that can enhance every moment of our lives: It's not something to be held in reserve to come to our rescue when we are in a crisis, although certainly it will be very helpful during difficult times. Here's everything you'll need in one table to create your own sustainable MAPP:

CREATING A SUSTAINABLE MINDFUL AWARENESS PRACTICE PLAN (MAPP)	
Who?	You. Show up. Your sincere intention. Commit.
Why?	Know your motivations. What has meaning for you?
When?	Discover your optimal practice time. Day or night.
Where?	Create your space. Almost any place will work.
What?	Determine your "way in." Just do it.
How?	Staple it. Connect it to something you are already doing regularly. Small steps.
How long?	12–15 minutes daily.

How can I be so sure that this plan will work for you? Because you are the designer of its every feature, and so far every student in my workshops has left with a plan! You have a standing invitation to give it a try—whenever you are ready to commit.

The first question is **Who?** It all starts with you, your intention, and your ability to commit now or whenever the time comes. Gretchen Rubin, author and self-proclaimed "happiness bully," says that when she sets an intention, such as jogging every week, she doesn't go week by week making that decision over and over. She sets it up to repeat weekly. That way it's just one decision. This can be especially effective for those of us who may find ourselves facing all kinds of pushback in the morning, such as *no time to work out today, it's raining,* or *I'm too busy.* If that one decision has been set, we're more likely to honor our intention. Rubin also schedules with a weekly running partner, her "outside motivator." For those of us who do best when we must be accountable to someone, the outside motivator can make the difference between following through or failing to do so.

The second question is **Why?** What is your reason for taking on a MAPP at this time? Knowing your own motivations, which are the only ones that matter here, will allow you to fully commit. This will include exploring what has meaning for you right now in your life. We'll be talking more about that in the part on Purpose. Once you have embraced the commitment, you can not only begin more easily but sustain your practice.

The third question is **When?** There are three aspects of *when*: First, if you are new to mindfulness and want to begin a practice, it will help to select a time to begin that will fit into not only your schedule but your life right now. In this way, you will be giving yourself the best chance of starting and sustaining a practice. As I've mentioned, many of us think most seriously about starting or resuming a practice when we really need it, such as when we receive an alarming medical diagnosis or during our busiest season at work. Consider starting at a time when you are not in crisis mode, at a time when you have the mental space to do so. Setting your intention is the starting point, and it's important to be "all in" so that you can truly commit.

Second, we all have an optimal time, whether it's during the day or night, when we would prefer to practice. Although that may change over time, at least initially, it can help to have the same time slot each day to the greatest extent possible. For me, the best time is first thing in the morning, when I feel refreshed and before anything can get in the way.

Third, there may be time in your day that you could repurpose to become your practice time. For example, you could do a mindfulness practice during your daily commute on the train or while walking your dog.

Then there's the question of **Where?** The place can vary from day to day, although most practitioners find that having a designated space, such as a quiet area in your home, is helpful in being consistent. However, it's also helpful to be open to other places so that you can practice where and when you may most need it during a given day. Blackburn practices what she calls *micro-meditations* at times that otherwise would leave her bored or impatient, such as waiting for a plane to take off or during a shuttle ride en route to a meeting.

The next question is **What?** Mindfulness can meet you where you are. *Start where you are.* You have the opportunity to "right-size" your practice. What resonates with you? Maybe it's yoga, mindful walking in the woods, or a sitting meditation practice.

What works for you one day, or one week, may not work the next. What works for your work colleagues may not work for you. I encourage you to be patient with yourself as you find what works best for you. It's important that the app, the podcast, the audio recording or video, whatever you may choose, resonates with you. The teachers your friend favors may not be the ones that make sense for you. The recording you listen to for three weeks may not be the one you choose to continue. The key is to figure out your own "way in" and adjust or change it as needed, knowing that your practice will evolve over time.

One other thing to keep in mind is that your mind isn't the same day to day. Picture your mind as a stream—it's similar day to day mostly, but it's never exactly the same. You may think that over time, your mind will stop wandering or become empty. Although it won't become empty, it will become clearer so that you will in time be less likely to be carried away by distractions.

Then there's the question of **How?** In my workshops on creating a sustainable mindfulness practice plan, the prospect of "stapling" the practice to something currently in the daily routine is one of the features that brings students the most optimism and satisfaction. Their plans have varied from arriving at the office ten minutes early to taking a break in the local park after their morning car pool for school. At a recent workshop, Carly mentioned that she has a sporadic schedule and fast-paced life, but her pet lizard, Ruby, relies on her to turn her light on each morning and off each night. So, Carly intends to staple her practice time to one of those two times. The last thing we need is one more thing on our already too long to-do lists, so attaching our meditation to something that is already part of our daily routine seems to work well for many of us.

Finally, **How long?** Research is inconclusive, but durations of nine, twelve, twenty, twenty-three, and thirty minutes daily have all been shown to provide positive results. Amishi Jha's research consistently finds that twelve to fifteen minutes is a sweet spot for a "minimum effective dose" for change to occur in time-pressured groups, such as first responders and the military. Mindfulness leader Sharon Salzberg advises, "I usually pad it and say twenty minutes, or more if you can." Experiment for yourself and see what works best for you.

The impact of dividing up your sessions into smaller periods is still being studied. Researchers at the University of Wisconsin are asking what's better—twenty minutes at a stretch, two ten-minute segments, or four five-minute segments? Science suggests that consistency is as important as, if not more important than, duration, so even a few minutes each day is better than waiting a couple of days until you hope you will have more time. Regularity is key, so even if it's just one minute a day, try doing it every day. Some find it helpful to use an app that keeps track of their "streaks" (the number of consecutive days).

If one to five minutes per day is your maximum right now, then that is your optimal starting point. Begin where you are. It may also help to shift your focus from how much time you spend meditating to how much mindfulness you bring into your everyday life. Ask yourself frequently, "What's my ability to be and remain present?" As discussed earlier, it's important to incorporate and appreciate informal as well as formal ways of cultivating Presence, as both provide benefits.

TIPS FOR STARTING AND SUSTAINING YOUR MINDFUL AWARENESS PRACTICE PLAN (MAPP)

- Select a date and time to start when you can truly commit.

- Know why this plan is important to you.

- If you discontinue your practice, remember, you can always begin again.

- Believe in yourself. You can do this.

~~~~~~

Presence in Brief

There is a burgeoning, worldwide interest in mindfulness and bringing it to industry and education, but you don't need anything fancy or extra to practice the skill of Presence. You have all that you need right now.

I have included an "In Brief" section at the end of each of the four parts of this book. As a lawyer, I've spent years writing legal briefs for the court that were anything but brief! I assure you that I have kept all of the "In Brief" sections intentionally short!

Presence is a way of life. It's neither a special tool nor a quick fix. It extends beyond formal practices, including yoga and sitting meditation, for example, to informal ones, such as being fully present for ordinary, everyday events such as drinking your tea or talking with friends. It sounds simple: Presence is being aware right now of what's going on by paying attention without getting carried away by judgment and with kindness for self and others. Well . . . actually . . . maybe that doesn't sound so simple . . . especially when we consider how increasingly distracting our world is and how our minds work, with countless, repetitive thoughts and judgments daily, largely about the past or future. So it takes mental training, as in both formal and informal practices, to increase Presence for optimal well-being.

Presence

being aware

right now

by paying attention

without getting carried away by judgment

with kindness for self and others

Practice Tips for All Meditations

You will find two mindfulness meditations at the end of each of the book's four parts. I invite you to try them out and select the ones that work best for you; many of them require just one to three minutes. When it comes to meditation, we all start at different baselines, with varied strengths and challenges. One size doesn't fit all. If any one of the practices resonates with you, I encourage you to use it throughout your day and notice how you feel at the end of the day. Try to repeat this daily for one week. As with our physical workouts, different exercises appeal to us on different days, so don't give up if what you chose one day isn't what you want to do the next. It's fun to mix it up. And remember, there's no one right way.

Before we get to the first practice, I'd like to share the story of Barbara and a few practice tips. Barbara, a full-time social worker for her county, has two teenage daughters and two young stepsons from her recent marriage. In her direct, earnest way Barbara told me that she was firmly convinced for years that meditation was "not her thing"; she considered herself the "last person on earth" to be interested. Two years ago, as a single parent with a crushing workload, she realized how short-fused she had become both at work and at home. She started going to a meditation group at her local college but found that it was too hard to attend in person with her hectic work schedule. Fortunately, the college offered a few meditations online and she was able to find a teacher with whom she resonated.

In the last year Barbara has set aside at least ten minutes daily to meditate. She was eager to describe for me how meditation has changed her life: "I'm no longer the little general, a complete mess who runs around screaming and angry." She explains that just taking one breath has provided her with the time needed between stimulus and response so that she can control her quick temper: *"The most important, surprising, crucial thing for someone who was volatile and reactive like I was is that you can change. That has been incredible. It's something you have to commit to. You don't understand how beneficial it's going to be; it's so hard to be consistent daily, but so well worth it."*

If Barbara can do this, so can you.

Just one more thing. Each one of us is unique and we may have different or unexpected responses to what may seem like a simple practice. So when anyone invites you to do a mindfulness practice, be sensitive to the fact that it may be an uncomfortable experience for you at this time, and you may need to modify the exercise. For example, someone who has had a near-drowning experience may have an adverse response to a breath awareness exercise because it may remind them of a distressing experience that they haven't yet resolved. In that case, you may want to make a modification and select a neutral focus, such as your hands or a candle.

PRACTICE POINTERS FOR ALL MEDITATIONS

* Know that your attention will wander, no matter which practice you choose, even within a very brief time frame, and even with your best intention to stay focused.

* Gently, consistently, and continuously bring your attention back to your breath or other object of your attention.

* Consider sounds to be touchstones for bringing your attention back, not interruptions to your meditation.

* Be patient and kind with yourself. No need to berate yourself.

- Remember, as soon as you become aware that you are distracted, you can refocus your attention and begin again.

- Celebrate. Being present for just one breath is a cause for celebration. Don't miss it.

~~~~~~

Breath Practices for Stress Reduction

We've been talking about how stress is an inherent part of a meaningful life so the key is how we relate to stress. Take a moment now to bring to mind a stressful situation. Perhaps you just received news about an ambiguous, scary result from a biopsy, or your company has just announced it's relocating, or your daughter just fell off the swings at the school playground. We each experience stress in a different way—some may say like "a weight on my chest," "a knot in my stomach," or "a pounding heart." Breathing exercises have been used for thousands of years in the yogic tradition to obtain certain positive physiological responses. Even the shortest, simplest mindful breathing exercises can produce results you will notice immediately. Why is that? Because the way we control our breathing is by regulating our autonomic nervous system, which helps us to create a state of calm.

For example, one form of breath practice involves altering the ratio of duration of inhaling and exhaling. *Whenever we exhale for longer than we inhale, our body goes into a state of relaxation.* The next time you have a difficult phone call to make, or have two hungry, out-of-sorts children on your hands, try this breath practice: Breathe in for four seconds and out for seven seconds. This is sometimes called the 4–7 Breath Practice.

Studies also show that simply being aware of the sensation of the breath helps calm the mind, even without controlling it as described above. This form of breath practice involves focusing attention on sensing the in breath and out breath. Noticing the cool air as you inhale and the warm air as you exhale may help you to stay focused on your breath, one breath at a time. This is sometimes called the Cool–Warm Breath Practice. You may prefer to focus on the movement of the abdomen in and out or the whole body breathing.

Be with what's happening right now. Continue this for one or two minutes, or longer if your time allows. Repeat as needed throughout your day. Notice how you feel both during and after these simple breath practices. You will likely notice your body relaxing. You will also likely feel calmer and confident that you can now better handle the challenge before you. Remember the Practice Pointers previously mentioned—your mind will likely wander and that's OK.

The important thing is to bring your attention back to your breath. When you realize your mind has wandered, you have become aware of what has distracted you—that is, what is in your awareness. Great! Now it's time to redirect your focus of attention back to the breath. Not to get too technical here, but redirecting your focus of attention means letting go of the distraction, and then focusing on the breath. For some people, naming the general kind of distraction helps (for example, "thinking," "remembering," or "feeling").

4–7 BREATH PRACTICE FOR STRESS REDUCTION

- Get into a comfortable yet dignified position, with eyes closed or gaze averted.

- Bring your awareness to your breath.

- Breathe in for a count of four, sensing your breath.

- Breathe out for a count of seven, sensing your breath.

- Repeat for one or two minutes anytime, as needed and as your time allows.

Quieting the Inner Critic Practice

We've talked about our inner critic, so now is a good time to introduce a mindfulness practice called Quieting the Inner Critic, which I've adapted from the work of mindfulness leader Sharon Salzberg.

QUIETING THE INNER CRITIC PRACTICE

1. Get into a comfortable, yet dignified posture, with eyes closed or gaze averted.

2. Call to mind a distressing emotion you've felt recently. Fear? Anger? Something else?

3. Notice how you feel about this emotion. Do you dislike yourself for it? Do you feel you should have been able to prevent it from arising? Are you ashamed of it?

4. Change the word *bad* to *painful*. Recognize that the difficult feeling is a painful state. See what happens to your relationship to that feeling when you reframe it.

5. Observe how that emotion feels in your body once you begin to hold it with some kindness and compassion. Observe the

various sensations; the pain is there and compassion surrounds it.

6. If the sense of *bad* comes back, and you catch yourself being critical and hard on yourself, replace that with compassion for yourself.

7. Reflect on the fact that you cannot prevent negative feelings from arising. You don't need to be overcome by them, act on them, or feel ashamed if you have them. Recognize that this is the nature of things, for ourselves as well as others.

8. Commit to noticing negative feelings more quickly, recognizing their painful nature, having compassion for yourself, and letting go.

9. When you are ready, slowly open your eyes.

PART 2

Presence and Purpose

Success is liking yourself, liking what you do,
and liking how you do it.
—MAYA ANGELOU

THE FIRST P IS PURPOSE, which provides us with a sense of meaning in our lives. Twenty-three hundred years ago, Aristotle asked: "What's the ultimate *purpose* of human activity?" His conclusion was happiness, but a certain kind of happiness that comes from the realization of our own true potential, our unique capacities, what he called the *daimon*. Aristotle contrasted a self-transcending state of *eudaimonia*, a state of human flourishing from pursuing long-term goals that give purpose to life (which I'll be talking about here), with self-enhancing *hedonia*, the short-term happiness that delivers a jolt of dopamine.

Of course, there was no science available then to test Aristotle's assertion—no randomized trials or fMRIs. Research has now shown that our bodies prefer selfless, eudaimonic happiness, which is about hard work and purposeful engagement. Though it entails efforts that may be stressful in the short term, over the long run eudaimonic happiness positively impacts our overall physical health in more ways than does the more self-enhancing hedonia. As Sanjiv Chopra and Gina Vild explain in *The Two Most Important Days*, "If you try to chase happiness without having a clear idea of what happiness is, you are destined to fail because you tend to pursue things that are ephemeral and provide only short-term pleasure. *When you approach happiness with an understanding that it is connected to purpose and to contributing in some way to the betterment of those around you, you will succeed. . . .* Here it is in four simple words: happiness is a choice" (italics mine).

Why would our bodies prefer Purpose, deferred gratification, and all of the effort of eudaimonia? One theory, according to psychiatry professor Steve Cole, is that if most of our happiness is derived from hedonic well-being, then when things don't go well and we feel unhappy, it threatens everything we derive our sense of happiness from. On the other hand, if what we value and work toward is a cause, in service of others and something bigger than ourselves, then bad events don't threaten us as much because our value lies in a Purpose that will live on and continue beyond our lifetime.

Purpose researcher William Damon, in his book *The Path to Purpose*, states: "Purpose endows a person with joy in good times and resilience in hard times, and this holds true all throughout life." Our lives are complex and nuanced, and we all have difficult, discouraging, and stressful days, but Purpose can keep us going during our most challenging times.

. . . .

Happiness is a choice.

—SANJIV CHOPRA AND GINA VILD

Here's an example of Purpose from behavior scientist Victor Strecher's conversation with Natalie Stavas, a pediatrician at Boston Children's Hospital. She was running the Boston Marathon in 2013 and was within eight hundred yards of the finish line when she heard a loud explosion accompanied by screams. In that split second, while most people were running away from the blast area, Natalie ran toward it. She jumped over race barriers in order to treat four victims—three of whom survived. She was hailed as a hero by President Barack Obama, but she feels that her actions were nothing special—just a reflection of who she is. Ironically, even for those whose callings might potentially put their own lives at risk, having a sense of Purpose keeps them happier and healthier overall.

What Is Purpose?

Let's start with the definition that is commonly used in the psychology literature: "Purpose is a central, self-organizing life aim that organizes and stimulates goals, manages behaviors, and provides a sense of meaning." I know. That's how researchers talk. Let's break it down. Think of the first feature, a "life aim," as an *ultimate concern* or *general intention*. It's the answer to questions such as "What matters most to you, and why?" and "What gets you out of bed in the morning?"

The second feature, "organizes and stimulates goals," refers to how having Purpose provides goals for us. I'm not referring to just any goals, but to our broad, valued, noble, or *higher-order* goals that are central to our identity and infused with personal meaning that energizes us. A valued goal need not be grand or global in order to increase our well-being; however, it does motivate us to do something that will have a consequence beyond ourselves. Damon explains that our Purpose need not be heroic, requiring life-endangering adventures, but may "*be found in the day-to-day fabric of ordinary existence.*" Examples of Purpose would include a mother caring for her child, a citizen campaigning for a candidate for the sake of improving the community, and a teacher instructing students. Dedicating time, care, and effort to charity, friends, family, communities, and our workplaces are other examples. Our valued goals are different than the specific goals that provide a way to pursue our Purpose, such as getting the education we need or setting up a recycling program in our neighborhood.

The third feature, "manages behaviors," means that Purpose provides a life's direction toward our valued goals, which in turn guides our daily efforts. This requires wisely allocating our finite personal resources (think time and attention).

Finally, the fourth feature of Purpose, a "sense of meaning," refers to a life worth living. We all likely know examples of people who have dropped out of business, law, medicine, the military, and other seemingly "solid careers"—they hadn't failed in the eyes of the world, but they felt they were failing themselves miserably. Why? They never had the sense that they were doing something that really mattered to them or the world. As Damon puts it, "Often it is the people who seem to be most on track who express the most severe misgivings." Damon's definition of purpose makes clear the importance of having a Purpose that reaches out to the world beyond ourselves, implying a desire to make a difference in the world: "*Purpose is a stable and generalized intention to accomplish something that is at the same time meaningful to the self and consequential for the world beyond the self.*"

Shirley was enjoying her life as a dancer and singer when at age nineteen she received a diagnosis of osteogenic sarcoma and was told that she had three to six months to live. She ultimately had to have her leg amputated. Shirley said that for years she would fill up her pant leg with stuffed pantyhose and put a shoe on it, until she joined a meditation group at her local church and was finally able, after five years, to come to terms with what had happened. During her hospitalization she had observed that some nurses weren't very caring and didn't want to talk to patients with terminal illnesses, and even placed them farthest from the nursing stations. This motivated Shirley to become a nurse and she found her Purpose in caring for her patients in the way that she wished she had been cared for. To this day, thirty years later, Shirley has a meditation practice and does yoga.

Purpose can center us, provide direction, energize and motivate us—all of which provide meaning to our daily lives. Purpose also gives us satisfaction when we accomplish our goals, and persistence when we run into obstacles. If your life is like mine, at the end of a hectic day full of surprises, setbacks, and putting out fires, as my former litigation colleagues would say, it's not unusual to focus most on what didn't get done. Having a Purpose focuses us on what matters most and keeps us moving toward accomplishing our Purpose so that we can feel fulfilled by our lives rather than defeated and drained, especially when we face setbacks and challenges.

You may be wondering if there's a difference between meaning and Purpose. The concepts of meaning and Purpose are intertwined and often used interchangeably. However, in the psychology literature they are separate constructs. Purpose refers to having direction and is more goal oriented, although what's personally meaningful drives our Purpose. Meaning in life, on the other hand, is often considered to have three facets: one's life having value or significance, having Purpose in life, and one's life being coherent as in "making sense." It's very hard for me as a perfectionist to write on any topic without getting completely carried away, but suffice it to say that Purpose provides meaning and direction for our lives, and what is personally meaningful to us informs our life's Purpose.

Living with awareness of our Purpose in life is living with Presence. It's the opposite of living on autopilot. Researchers Frank Martela and Michael Steger describe it this way: "The effectiveness of a given purpose relies upon its scope, its strength, and its presence in people's awareness." It's not uncommon to live on autopilot for years, perhaps in pursuit of goals that once made sense for us but no longer do. Presence is key to getting in touch with what's meaningful to us right now.

Presence and Purpose can center us when our expectations aren't met or when some other challenge arises. Here's an example from my own life. A few years ago, I was returning from a business trip after several days and was looking forward to going for a walk with our son, Alex, as soon as I got home. But when I arrived, he didn't want to go out for a walk; he preferred to draw on his newsprint pad. I had an image of the imagined future that was not to be, so fortunately I took a moment to get back in touch with the present—and with my larger Purpose. Once I took another moment to reconnect to my Purpose—to be an engaged and loving parent—I could feel more at ease. After a few minutes, I felt much calmer and we both enjoyed drawing and hanging out together at home.

Seeking versus Having a Purpose in Life

Within the psychology literature on Purpose or meaning, two components are discussed: (a) search for, and (b) presence of. The reason for this is that they are associated with different outcomes for different age groups. The *search* for Purpose is usually associated with well-being primarily in adolescence and early adulthood (which research shows spans more years than ever before—perhaps into our early thirties), and at any age during times of transition in our lives, whereas the *presence* of Purpose is associated with well-being across the life span. Research suggests that adolescents and young adults need only to feel that they have the will (as in the drive or motivation) to reach their ultimate aim; that is, they don't need to believe they know how to go about doing so in order to feel satisfied with their lives. That changes later in young adulthood, however, when the relationship between Purpose and life satisfaction is mediated by the belief that *we have the will and know the way to reach our ultimate aim.* Simply put, *by adulthood it becomes important to have not only a will but a way for achieving one's goals in life.* Not surprisingly, studies confirm that *high levels of search for Purpose and meaning with low levels of Presence are associated with more anxiety and general stress.*

As we all hopefully enjoy longer health spans, there's more likelihood and opportunity than ever before that we will find ourselves searching for new Purposes in life well beyond adolescence and young adulthood. Many of us will have several careers and more than one partner or family during our longer life spans. We will also have more opportunity to pursue new interests and undertake projects that will provide meaning for us. When we make these life changes—and we will talk more about changes in Part 3 on Pivoting—we will likely find ourselves seeking a new Purpose, which will ultimately need to be accompanied by our not only finding that Purpose but having a way to realize it. One study of "9-enders" (individuals ending a decade, at ages twenty-nine, thirty-nine, forty-nine, etc.) found that since they tend to focus more on aging, they likely reported more searching for meaning in life. Why not always harbor this dynamic mentality?

Merely having a Purpose, that is, the presence of Purpose, is not enough. What accounts for feeling a sense of well-being is having the ability to take steps—or to at least know the steps that we can take—to connect us to our Purpose. In other words, we need to have a plan, or take action, in the direction of fulfillment of our Purpose.

Coherence is an aspect of meaning that scientists also call our *autobiographical narrative*. It basically means making sense of our lives, or knowing our life story. We are always trying to know and make sense of our own narrative. After all, we are called *Homo sapiens sapiens*, the ones who "know and know we know." We could, however, just as accurately be called the ones who tell stories. Knowing our narrative helps us make sense of both where we've been and where we're going; it ties together our sense of self from past, present, and future. Once we become aware of our own story, we can begin to realize and appreciate our unique potential, move out of our own way, and embrace our Purpose in life.

What's Your Story?

Figuring out your life story starts with looking to your past and future. This is the kind of intentional mental time travel I mentioned earlier that serves us well. We can't fully live in the present without having harnessed this amazing ability our brains have to look at our past in order to understand how it relates to our present and future. We are all lugging past burdens around with us. Counterintuitive as it may seem, *to be fully in the present, we need to have a solid command of not only our past but also our anticipated future.* Purpose helps us make sense of where we've been and where we are going, tying together our sense of past, present, and future self.

It's only in looking at our past that we can truly make sense of our lives. As Steve Jobs said, "You can't connect the dots looking forward; you can only connect them looking backwards. So, you have to trust that the dots will somehow connect in your future. You have to trust in something—your gut, destiny, life, karma, whatever." As we look back at our lives, seemingly disparate parts are often seen to be connected to a thread, a self-organizing central aim, a Purpose. It is that which we gravitate toward and value that connects our narrative and within which we find our meaning and Purpose in life. Take a moment right now to think about two or three chapters of your own life that didn't seem to fit together at the time, but now in hindsight you can see how they may be related, or coherent.

If we have not been able to make sense of our life experiences, including our early life, then our narrative will feel fragmented. This is important because the past could be limiting our perspective when it comes to anticipating the future; we sometimes live with an imprisoning perspective. Making sense of the past is essential to being free of judgments in the present and being liberated for our future so that we may continue to live consistent with our Purpose.

My life story began on a working dairy farm in the village of Darien, Wisconsin, population 803 (700 of which are cows, Dan likes to point out). My parents were fourth-generation dairy farmers. I was the oldest of four, followed by two brothers, and then finally— my dream come true—a baby sister. My mom had lots of rules, one of which to my chagrin was boys outside, girls inside. However, I did have one delightful, daily outside job: going to the henhouse to collect and count the eggs.

While I was a junior in high school, a telegram arrived at our farmhouse one spring day stating, "Caroline Welch has been placed with a family in Shiraz, Iran, for the summer as part of our American Field Service Program." I hadn't mentioned the program to my parents, thinking I was unlikely to be selected, so why stir things up? They were alarmed, and once the news set in, we pulled the *Encyclopedia Britannica* off the shelf, located Iran on the map, and started learning about the country my parents knew as Persia. No one in my family had ever been on an airplane, so the idea of my flying to Tehran, picking up and dropping off exchange students along the way in New York, Istanbul, and Beirut, was terrifying. In the end, my parents allowed me to go, my dad took a couple of calves to market to cover the airfare, and off I went for a summer that changed my life.

Certainly when I left for Iran, I wasn't thinking about how this experience would fit into my life's Purpose, but in hindsight, I have been able to connect quite a few dots. There have been several adventures all along the way, and looking back I can see that one of my life's Purposes from early on has been lifelong learning. I was aware upon returning from Iran that I learned more that summer than in all of my previous years in school. That led to my continuing to seek out new challenges in diverse environments, from being one of four white students attending the historically black Grambling State University in Louisiana, working in Japan for three years, and visiting other countries. Now I've come full circle, starting with my introduction to meditation in Japan forty years ago to the Purpose of my work today at the Mindsight Institute to synthesize and summarize the latest science on mindfulness for practical application in our lives. It's almost as if I had a plan, but I didn't. Nonetheless, as with your own life's undertakings and experiences, in reviewing them you will likely find a connection that now makes sense.

The Health Benefits of Purpose

We are all familiar with the health risks of tobacco use, poor diet, inactivity, bad stress, and other lifestyle factors that contribute to roughly half of disease and early death, but have you heard anything about the health risks associated with an absence of Purpose or meaning in life? Current research shows that a lack of Purpose in our lives is contributing at least as much to our disease and premature death as these other factors.

Imagine a new drug on the market that makes us robust so that we will live longer, enjoy a happier old age, better retain our memory, and be more likely to not only survive a scary diagnosis but thrive. Sound too good to be true? Interested in knowing more? As it turns out, it isn't a new miracle drug; it's Purpose. Research shows that some of the health benefits of living with Purpose include adding years to our lives, reducing the risk of heart attack and stroke, cutting the risk of Alzheimer's disease by more than half, repairing our chromosomes, increasing good cholesterol and helping us to relax during the day and sleep better at night.

Research on meaning and Purpose has its roots in the experiences of the Viennese psychiatrist Viktor Frankl, Holocaust survivor and concentration camp prisoner #119104. Frankl detailed his experiences in his memoir, *Man's Search for Meaning*, and is widely credited with bringing attention to meaning in life in psychology with his development of logotherapy (*meaning therapy*). In the concentration camps, Frankl noticed that his fellow prisoners who had a sense of meaning showed greater resilience to torture, slave labor, and starvation than those who did not have a sense of meaning. He found some explanation for this in the words of Friedrich Nietzsche to the effect that those who have a *why* to live can bear almost any *how*.

A strong sense of Purpose is also associated with greater meaning in life, happiness, self-esteem, and the ability to view goal pursuits as challenges rather than threats. Furthermore, as journalist Barbara Hagerty points out in *Life Reimagined*, "*Purpose in life is more important than education or wealth in determining long-term health and happiness*" (italics mine). And no matter our age, with Purpose, we have the ability to process negative information in a more positive way because we are better able to view life's challenges within a larger context.

Purpose in Our Work

A study at the University of Michigan Health System assessed sense of purpose in hospital cleaners and found that those who felt part of the medical team showed greater job satisfaction and a deeper psychological connection to their work. There is a relationship between how coworkers make individuals feel about their work and the individuals' sense of self-worth. Not just in hospitals, but in workplaces in general, individuals appreciate recognition and being valued as part of a larger team.

I encountered several examples from women around the world who had switched jobs in order to have more Purpose in their work. In Istanbul, I interviewed three women, all of whom now work for a major hospital and previously had careers in advertising, hospitality, and finance, respectively. One woman, Beyza, described the difference she experiences in her new position this way: "I was feeling claustrophobic at the bank . . . now everyone around me is trying to change something that really matters to our patients. It's a different world. I'm feeding my soul through my work, which has never been possible before."

Many of the women whom I interviewed from dual-career families talked about the necessary trade-off between work and home life. What I heard consistently is that "some things just have to slide," and the most important thing is that the kids be happy and safe. Shannon and her wife both work and have two school-aged kids. Shannon's consulting business requires that she travel out of town at least once a month. Upon returning from a recent trip, Shannon was able to keep herself from asking her wife why the apartment was such a mess. She kept in mind that their kids were doing great, and that is what's most important to her.

When I asked Rhonda Magee, law professor and leader in the field of inclusive pedagogy, about her Purpose in life, she said that she sees it two ways. On a micro level, having experienced trauma early in life, her Purpose is to further her own healing, but she quickly added, "I've always felt very clear that my life was not meant to be just for myself and that whatever I might learn about healing would be something that I could offer and would in any case be of benefit to others."

Magee went on to explain that on a macro level, her Purpose revolves around the work she does to provide doorways into mindfulness for those whom she teaches and to make our various communities more inclusive. In addressing organizations around the United States, Magee has noticed an increased awareness on the part of not only minority groups but members of the majority population as well, of the importance of supporting more diversity and inclusiveness, an "ethical call for more awareness on everyone's part" to use her words.

Triona in Belfast, Northern Ireland, had her own event-planning business for years before she turned to organizing conferences that address trauma, a very relevant topic in her home country of Northern Ireland. She grew up in the Catholic section of Belfast and vividly remembers her parents' routine of calling the military to do a controlled explosion whenever there was an abandoned car in front of their home, which was often. During the explosions, she and her siblings would be moved to a windowless room in the rear of their house, shielded from shattering windows. Her story isn't unique among the Northern Irish. When I asked Triona about how her family and others coped with this, she said, "The attitude is to pull your socks up and get on with it. Asking for help is asking for a crutch. My mom said if she ever thought about the trauma or even started talking about it, she would never stop crying." Triona explained that as she has allowed herself over time to reflect upon her own trauma, she has become increasingly motivated and excited to align her work with a field that provides Purpose for her. The impetus for the shift in her work came from within, and Triona took it upon herself to make a change. We'll talk more about Pivoting, or making changes, in Part 3.

Mimi Guarneri, or "Dr. G" as nicknamed by her patients, is a fifty-eight-year-old cardiologist who heads up her own integrative medical center in La Jolla, California. Dr. G made being a cardiologist and serving her patients her life's Purpose. During medical school, when others would try to dissuade her and encourage her to choose a potentially less demanding specialty, she held steadfast to her life's Purpose of being a cardiologist. Dr. G talked about what she calls "the golden cage" (also commonly called "the gilded cage"), which can keep all of us hard at work around the clock supporting a lifestyle that we may have little, if any, time to enjoy.

When I asked Dr. G how she managed to escape her golden cage, she explained that at age forty she found herself putting in about seven hundred stents a year and over time her focus moved from intervention to prevention. She observed that nothing was being done to "turn off the faucet," that is, to help patients never return to the hospital. Realizing that, she said to herself: *"I'd rather fail at my own work than be successful at doing someone else's."* Presence has also been a large part of Dr. G's life, as she has had a meditation practice of her own for decades and encourages her patients to have one as well. As she puts it, *"Make meditation your medicine."*

....

> *Ever more people today have the means to live,*
> *but no meaning to live for.*
>
> —VIKTOR FRANKL

Dispelling the Myths

You may be thinking that the health benefits of Purpose, as well as the examples you've read, all sound good, but you aren't yet convinced that having a Purpose is within your reach. It may seem daunting. I'll be dispelling three of the most common myths about Purpose, as identified by researcher Heather Malin in *Teaching for Purpose*:

MYTH #1: *Purpose requires passion.* A popular mantra or message that is likely familiar to you is "Find your passion;" and it's often offered not only to young adults, but throughout our lives. However, our Purpose need not be something we are passionate about. That doesn't mean that our Purpose isn't what matters most to us, it just means that it can be uncoupled from passion. Innovators Bill Burnett and Dave Evans found that *80 percent of people of all ages are unable to identify a passion but are still able to pursue a purposeful path* (italics mine). So you need not find something you are passionate about in order to have Purpose. Of course, you may find that you are passionate about what constitutes Purpose for you, as the two concepts are not mutually exclusive. Malin explains that although it's great if our Purpose is something we're passionate about, ". . . it does not have to be experienced at that level of intensity, or narrowed to a single, consuming interest. . . . The flame of purpose, once ignited, burns steadily and acts as a guiding light. It does not flash and burn out quickly, as passions often do."

MYTH #2: *Purpose is one and done.* We need not seek or have just one Purpose to last our entire lifetime. In fact, since we are often highly engaged simultaneously in many different roles or activities, we may not only have different purposes that may change over time, but add new ones. Nonetheless, it is in the nature of Purpose to endure at least long enough for us to commit to it by taking action, and usually to make progress toward accomplishing it.

Our capacity to change our life's Purpose as needed enables us to continue experiencing the benefits of a meaningful life, because having Purpose is not only exhilarating but also motivating for further lifelong learning. Often Pivoting or making changes accompanies seeking and sustaining our Purpose as we move through life; we'll be talking about Pivoting in Part 3.

MYTH #3: *Purpose is a luxury, only for the privileged.* Like Presence, Purpose is a natural resource that is available to us 24/7, and it's free. No special equipment or resources are required in order to find Purpose in our lives, even if we are facing a challenge in life or struggling to make ends meet. In fact, Purpose can be especially helpful in seeing us through in times of hardship. Malin puts it this way: "Most positive psychologists argue that purpose is an important asset that supports resilience, thriving, and optimal development. If anything, purpose is most useful to those who face hardships, and *it should be encouraged as a necessity of life rather than a luxury*" (italics mine).

If any of these myths ring true for you, hopefully you can now take the first step in having Purpose, which is finding what matters most to you.

Finding Our Purpose in Life

When it comes to finding our Purpose, we first need to identify our values, which are influenced by a variety of factors—including our country, our education, the people around us, and people whom we admire. Purpose arises out of what provides meaning for us, what we value. The World Values Survey, a global research project that regularly studies values and beliefs, asked seventy thousand people from fifty-one countries to rank values, such as independence, wealth, security, pleasure, giving to society, helping others, the environment, and tradition. One of the consistently highest-ranking values across all countries and incomes was helping others.

Here are a few questions that might assist you in finding your purpose in life: *What's most important to you? What do you value in life? Who do you look up to?* and *What gets you up in the morning?* Considering the answers to these questions for the various roles you play will allow you to articulate your purpose and what matters most in your life.

We may not need to look too far for our Purpose as it's often found within a setting with which we are familiar. That's how it worked out for Peggy O'Kane, one of the most influential women in health care today who pioneered the evaluation of medical care plans. After five years as a respiratory therapist in a hospital, Peggy came to have a good understanding of what's wrong with our health care system and what needs to be done about it. She looked around and felt she had something to contribute in the field of quality assurance and realized that for this next phase of her career, her Purpose was to help employers and consumers evaluate health care plans. O'Kane says she was helped in setting up her company, since being neither a man nor a doctor, she was underestimated. Now, after thirty years in her field, Peggy has no plans to retire and has more fun every day.

On the other hand, Purpose may emerge through circumstances and changes that we never could have imagined. Just months before she passed away, I had the privilege of interviewing Marie Tsuruda, a gentle, soft-spoken, second-generation Japanese American in her mid-eighties with a twinkle in her eye but a little bit of sadness about her. Perhaps I sense this because I know of her internment at the Jerome War Relocation Center in Arkansas during World War II. Marie was one of the nearly 120,000 people of Japanese descent affected. Just days prior to the start of the war, her two older sisters went to Japan to visit their grandparents, and once the war broke out, they had to stay in Japan, separated from the rest of the family in California. Marie was just fifteen when the war ended, but she decided that she didn't want to live in a country that had interned her based on her ethnicity, so she decided to move to Japan to reunite with her sisters. Unbeknownst to Marie, her sisters were simultaneously making their way back to California.

Once in Japan, Marie was ostracized and not accepted as "real Japanese" since she was unfamiliar with the language, customs, and culture. She never felt like a part of Japanese society until she became an English teacher at the YMCA in Hiroshima, where she went on to become chair of the English department. Marie was the only native English speaker in the school when she arrived (now there are dozens, thanks to the burgeoning interest in English-as-a-second-language [ESL] education in Japan) and she felt like a queen: She was the expert! Finally she was home, and she had found one of her life's Purposes: to be the best English teacher she could be for her highly motivated students. Having taught in her department for three years, I know her students remain grateful for Tsuruda-sensei's inspirational teaching.

You may be thinking to yourself, "This is easier said than done; when am I supposed to find the time to find my Purpose?" Remember, it's not that you will be pulling it out of thin air; you will look at what is already in your life—your values, your goals, and what's meaningful to you—and go from there. When we do nothing about a cause we feel strongly about, we feel overwhelmed and powerless. On the other hand, once we get involved and take small steps, over time we find a sense of meaning and accomplishment. Remember, your Purpose can be changed, updated, expanded, contracted, or refined as you move through your life's stages. Purposes are not necessarily one and done, although they can be. And as mentioned earlier, we likely have a different Purpose for each of the various facets of our lives.

....

Life is never made unbearable by circumstances, but only by lack of meaning and purpose.

—VIKTOR FRANKL

The Top Five Regrets of the Dying

You may be wondering what dying has to do with seeking or having Purpose. Fast-forwarding to the end of our lives and considering what we don't want to regret is another way of illuminating our Purpose. Palliative care nurse Bronnie Ware identified these top five regrets of her end-of-life patients. Presence plays a central role in all of them.

> **Regret 1:** *I wish I'd had the courage to live a life true to myself, not the life others expected of me.*

Does this sound familiar? You may recall that in Part 1 on Presence, we discussed the importance of creating our own narratives, free to the greatest extent possible from expectations or judgments of others and ourselves. The key thing to keep in mind when seeking our Purpose is knowing and believing that the answers lie within us; we just need to give ourselves the time and space to consider what has meaning for us. That's not easy given how busy we are and how much we automatically rely on outside sources to guide us, including social media and Google. We'll be talking more about social media and the Internet in part 4.

Michelle Obama had the following thoughts about Barack a few months after they first met: "[His] inborn confidence was admirable, of course, but honestly, try living with it. For me, coexisting with Barack's strong sense of purpose—sleeping in the same bed with it, sitting at the breakfast table with it—was something to which I had to adjust, not because he flaunted it, exactly, but because it was so alive." She then wrote on the first page of her journal: "One, I feel very confused about where I want my life to go. What kind of person do I want to be? How do I want to contribute to the world? Two, I am getting very serious in my relationship with Barack and I feel that I need to get a better handle on myself." Around this same time, Michelle realized the following: "Somehow, in all my years of schooling, I hadn't managed to think through my own passions and how they might match up with work I found meaningful. *As a young person, I'd explored exactly nothing*" (italics mine). This may ring true for many of us as we often come to this important exploration later in life.

Regret 2: *I wish I hadn't worked so hard.*

This one may also sound familiar, as we've talked about not getting caught up in a single, all-consuming pursuit, such as our work, to the exclusion of other parts of our lives.

Regret 3: *I wish I'd had the courage to express my feelings.*

Our direct experience, our sensing, is crucial and can only happen when we are in a state of Presence, in those moments when we manage to step out of our thought loops and get in touch with our senses. Accessing our feelings is the first step in expressing them.

Regret 4: *I wish I had stayed in touch with my friends.*

It isn't easy to maintain our friendships especially when we are in the midst of demanding years pursuing our careers, raising children, or tending to any of the other often all-consuming responsibilities we have. Bronnie Ware summarizes the value of friends this way: "History and understanding are what friendships offer. Life gets busy, and friendships fade away. There will always be people who come and go in life, friends included. But those who truly matter, those whom you love most dearly, are worth every ounce of effort to stay in touch with." Science now confirms the importance of maintaining our friendships for our health and well-being. Loneliness is more harmful to our well-being than smoking. In fact, *not having strong social connections represents a greater health risk than obesity and is as destructive to your health as smoking fifteen cigarettes a day.*

Regret 5: *I wish I had let myself be happier.*

We started our discussion on Purpose talking about a certain kind of happiness in which we enjoy a state of *eudaimonia*, or flourishing from pursuing long-term goals that provide Purpose to our lives. I trust that by this point in the book, you are getting a strong sense of how happiness is connected to Purpose. Happiness is a choice we can make. Our taking the time to get in touch with what's meaningful for us leads us to our Purpose, which is what ultimately makes us happy.

....

The most regretful people on earth are those who felt the call to creative work, who felt their own creative power restive and uprising, and gave to it neither power nor time.

—*MARY OLIVER*

Self-Care Is Not Selfish

There is another essential ingredient for having both Presence and Purpose in our lives that most of us hear a great deal about but aren't very good at—taking care of ourselves. I'm using *self-care* in its broadest, multidimensional sense—beyond haircuts and coffee breaks—to include our physical, mental, social, and spiritual well-being in order to accept support and love ourselves the way we do our dearest friends, through both positive and negative life events. I'm sure you're familiar with the mandate of putting on your own oxygen mask first in case of an emergency while flying. That's a great example of looking after yourself even though your first instinct, especially in an emergency, may be to help the person next to you, especially if you're with a child.

When I asked about self-care in my interviews, woman after woman answered along similar lines: "I haven't learned to do that yet," "I just can't do that; I'm not that person," and "If I'm not working, it's all about my family; I literally have no time for myself." Sound familiar? Some of you may not even get to feeling selfish because you're not on your own to-do list; morning to night consists of demands from work, kids, parents, spouse, friend in crisis, home, and whatever else needs to be done (in no particular order). By the end of your day, it's late and you're exhausted.

Some women, including Kelly, the psychotherapist and main breadwinner for her family whom I introduced earlier, have what they call "structured self-care." In Kelly's case this includes designated date nights with her husband, reading, swimming, and visiting her local farmer's market on weekends. What happens when we always put others first, and neglect to take care of ourselves? Mindfulness teacher Sharon Salzberg cautions that when we act generously, on the basis of feeling unworthy of self-care and self-compassion, we eventually become resentful. Salzberg encourages her students to look at their intentions and motivation for giving: "Taking care of others with resentment isn't generosity. We can't give endlessly. We need to take care of ourselves, to break and breathe."

Self-care includes following your dreams. Tanvi, a single mom with two teenage children, worked as the director of a weight loss surgery clinic in a major hospital in Connecticut and had promised herself when her children were born that she would go back to school to get her graduate degree in nursing. Finally it was time, and she worked out a child care share program with her neighbor and enrolled in the program of her dreams at her local university. She's now within six months of finishing her program and said the one thing that kept her going is knowing that with her advanced degree, she will be even more valuable to her patients.

Why not expand self-care to not only support you during the emergencies and the tough times, but also during your everyday, ordinary, as well as joyous times? What if you could find a dear friend to be with you not just when you are having a bad day but also when you are having a good day, someone to celebrate with you along the way? Good news: That dear friend happens to live with you—it's you!

Self-care is indispensable to fulfilling our Purpose in life; without it, we are of no use to others or ourselves. As Zen priest Joan Halifax says in *Standing at the Edge* about her years of work with those who were dying, she found herself "worn out and discouraged . . . [I had to] take care of myself. [I] would nap, walk in the mountains, read a book, meditate, or perhaps best of all, just be lazy and aimless. Essentially, [I] had to press the Restart button, which meant turning off the machine!"

Prioritizing self-care is necessary for our living with Presence and Purpose. When it comes to sleep, for example, research shows that senior executives get more sleep than lower-level managers, with no difference along gender lines. How did researchers make sense of this? They concluded that senior executives prioritize both discipline and self-care, recognizing the need for self-care and the impossibility of doing it all. It's important to let ourselves relax, not only for our personal well-being but also to thrive professionally.

Social Snacking

We've talked about our in-person relationships, but what about our virtual relationships? MIT professor Sherry Turkle has spent her life studying the effects of our 24/7 connectivity and describes in *Alone Together* how we are losing our ability to engage socially when it's appropriate to connect more intimately with someone. Canceling dinner with Grandma, for example, may best be done by a phone call, not a text or email.

Research supports a link between social media, specifically Facebook use, and loneliness. Lonely people are more drawn to the mediated communication that social media provides, and make a habit of what researchers call "social snacking," that is, the temporary but illusory fulfillment of social needs that social network sites allow through activities like status updates, lurking on others' profiles, or passively viewing Instagram feeds—all of which may increase loneliness. Social snacking may make you feel

Alone Together v. Together

as though your immediate social needs have been met, but these activities fail to contribute to interpersonal connection, ultimately resulting in a deficit in important relational resources such as social support. "Social snacking" can in no way substitute for the benefits we receive through real life, in-person social interactions.

As social beings with social brains, we look to others for affirmation and approval. That can make it difficult to ferret out what's meaningful for us—what our Purpose is. Think about the latest image you posted on social media and how happy you were to receive likes, comments, or reactions. I'm reminded of the tourists I saw in front of the Eiffel Tower a few years ago. They merely glanced at the tower, took pictures, posted them, and then spent almost an hour reviewing the comments and likes that were rolling in. This is how our social brain network operates—our reward system is very much tied to what others think.

We are never far from seeing what's going on with friends at our fingertips, thanks to our digital devices. We see only "super happy," polished, perfect people through the carefully curated lens of omnipresent social media platforms. Women are more likely than men to become addicted to using social media platforms. *Flawed photos don't get posted and those without enough likes get deleted.* Over 70 percent of us sleep with our phones, we're agitated if we misplace any one of our devices, and on average we swipe our phones 150 times a day. Our brains have literally become addicted to social media platforms, and as you read this, scientists are studying Social Media Disorder (SMD). Simultaneously, teams of tech experts are working around the clock to make sure that their platforms obtain and maintain as much of our attention as possible. Contemplate the last time you intended to just quickly check your favorite social media platform and then were shocked when you realized how much time had passed. The fact is that we will rarely—if ever—be able to beat the algorithms specifically designed to keep our attention for as long as possible. I'll be talking more about our use of technology in Part 4 on Pacing.

The Thief of All Joy: Comparison

A friend stopped by recently to share photos she had taken on a journey to Alaska. Before we started looking at the photos, I mentioned that our family had enjoyed a cruise to Alaska some years ago, to which my friend said: "Oh, no, we didn't want to take a cruise. We prepared the entire itinerary ourselves and went on land to Denali National Park, met up with friends, and did lots of great hiking." I immediately felt bad, despite having had a fantastic time in Alaska and over fifteen years of revisiting happy memories about our family's vacation! In one fell swoop, all of that vanished as I was suddenly feeling that our Alaska trip was not so great after all. How ridiculous is that?

Comparison is inherent in our social interactions, whether in

The Thief of All Joy: Comparison

person or online. Another aspect of our social brains is that we want to belong to a group, and we want to be treated as well as others in the group. That's wired in our brains. In one research study that illustrates how important it is for members of a group to be treated fairly, researchers taught capuchin monkeys to swap plastic tokens for food. Normally, the monkeys were content exchanging a token for cucumbers; however, the monkeys were triggered if they saw a neighbor getting a grape instead of a cucumber. In about half of the trials, the monkeys who received cucumbers instead of grapes either refused to hand over their tokens or rejected the cucumber altogether; some threw their tokens or cucumbers out of their cages in defiance.

Perhaps the next time you find yourself comparing and getting frustrated with yourself for comparing, you can give yourself a break, as this is part of being human. We all can remember times when we thought we had a good life until we heard about someone else's life or we hopped on Facebook and found our newsfeeds full of shiny snippets of others' lives. We thought we had a wonderful time at our birthday party, until we heard about our friend's birthday party. When it comes to social media, "everyone's killing it all the time." We are never far from seeing how others are seemingly doing much better and having more fun than we are.

Our social media platforms take comparison to another level because the basis of comparison is so much broader. Social comparison is no longer limited to the Joneses next door, your colleagues at the office, or friends *in real time*; it's all of those connections along with their pasts and presents, and droves of other acquaintances: so-called friends, followers, connections, matches, and likes, many of whom we'll never meet in person. Nonetheless, science confirms that these interactions can have an impact on us, which may be deeply disturbing and distracting since they can conjure up feelings of inadequacy and negativity deep within us. Not surprisingly, researchers found a link between depression and Facebook users who compare themselves to others.

As you likely know from your own experience, comparisons can consume us. Using Presence to first of all be aware of what thoughts or feelings we may be experiencing is the first step. Next is to appreciate the power of our social brains with their inherent capacity to compare, so that we may find and live with Purpose

without regard (as best we can) for what others around us may be
valuing and doing.

Differentiation + Linkage = Integration

Part of finding and having a Purpose is understanding and appreciating that each one of us is a collection of parts, aspects, facets, or
subpersonalities. It may help to think of it like this: We each have
differentiated parts, which when linked together can become integrated. We are integrated beings, a combination or joining of different parts, rather than a blend. When we are integrated, we feel
harmonious and can more easily move among the various roles we
play—career woman, graduate student, mom, friend, volunteer, to
name just a few—each with its own unique Purpose. The whole and
integrated self has an exponential quality; it is much greater than the
sum of its parts. With respect to each role, we have the capacity to
activate a state at 100 percent; for example, I am 100 percent writer
right now. In fifteen minutes, when my daughter, Maddi, texts, I
will be 100 percent mom (which is sometimes challenging for both
of us!).

The self is inherently indefinable, elusive, and ever-shifting. It's
composed of porous parts that hold our multiple roles and responsibilities, demanding that we move seamlessly from one to the other
as we strive to combine work, personal, and all other aspects of our
lives. Our roles are constantly shifting, which means our selves are
always changing. *We are morphing every minute.* And how could it
be otherwise? We all may not play the same roles, but we share the

multitude and diversity of our roles and responsibilities. My own roles include daughter, spouse, parent, aunt, cousin, teacher, student, attorney, author, business owner, teacher, speaker, caregiver, friend, mentor, mentee, volunteer, and lifelong learner. As Diane Ackerman puts it, "We are all shape-shifters and magical reinventors. Life is really a plural noun, a caravan of selves."

If we don't honor integration, we may experience chaos or rigidity. Getting consumed by your work, for example, and having it hijack your life, will likely leave you feeling one-dimensional. You may lose touch with your friendships, your family, and other aspects of your life that are important. On the other hand, you may be experiencing chaos because you can't seem to get anything done—you intend to finish a work project but then get distracted by family drama, the latest national news, or a push notification. You may feel out of control, as confusion and turmoil take over your day. This is when Presence and paying attention to what's going on, together with having and living consistent with your Purpose, is especially helpful as it can provide direction and goals for us, both of which arise out of what is personally meaningful for us. As I've mentioned earlier, each of the facets of our life may mean a different Purpose.

I had the good fortune of attending a workshop led by the late Irish poet John O'Donohue. One morning he posed a particularly provocative question to the group: "For those of you who are married, how much of you is married?" After an extended pause, a long discussion ensued as we explored what it means to have various parts of ourselves, requiring that we play several different roles, including new ones we hadn't anticipated. On the following page is a chart depicting the elements of integration.

INTEGRATION = DIFFERENTIATION + LINKAGE			
What Is Integration?	Recognizing features of the different parts of ourselves	Linking the parts without losing their distinctiveness	Combining, not blending, the parts into a whole
Imagine a Fruit Salad	Strawberries, bananas, and pineapple	. . . in a bowl	Combined for a fruit salad, not a smoothie

The Gift of Gratitude

The word *gratitude* is derived from the Latin root *gratia*, meaning grace, graciousness, or gratefulness. *Gratitude* is often defined as appreciating what we receive, whether tangible or intangible, but there's a wider definition that's useful here: Gratitude is acknowledging the goodness in our lives, appreciating what's valuable and meaningful to us, and being appreciative of experiences. Presence also plays an important role here because when we take time to express our thanks to others, we not only have become aware of what is most valuable to us, but we have communicated or shared our awareness with those around us.

Gratitude is a gateway to Purpose because it helps us figure out what has value and provides meaning in our lives. As the Dalai Lama reminds us, "Gratitude helps us catalog, celebrate, and rejoice in each day and each moment before they slip through the vanishing hourglass of experience." Purpose researcher William Damon expresses it this way: "From gratitude springs not only an enhanced appreciation for our own blessings but also a desire to pass such blessings along to others—the heart and soul of purpose." Studies show that gratitude is strongly and consistently correlated with greater happiness; it helps us feel more positive emotions, relish good experience, improve our health, cope with adversity, and build strong relationships.

With practice, we can develop the ability to notice and appreciate the bounty in our everyday lives. One way is a gratitude journal. A recent study divided participants into three groups and assigned each group a different task; the first group was instructed to journal about hassles and annoyances, the second group about the things they felt grateful for, and the third group about neutral life events. The second group had consistently higher well-being.

Take a moment to think about the things that you are grateful for in your life. Sometimes we can't even be fully grateful for what exists in our lives until we experience loss. Melissa, at sixty-two, works as the dean of students at her local junior college and says that her life has been "pretty uneventful" compared to others. She decided in her late twenties not to have children, and both her parents and her in-laws passed away at relatively young ages, so she hasn't had the caregiving responsibilities many do. One windy night, Melissa and her husband went to sleep in their suburban neighborhood in Santa Rosa, California, only to be awakened at 2 a.m. by a loud, persistent pounding. When she finally opened her front door, she said it was "like opening my oven door"; it was her neighbor, alerting her to the nearby hillside fire. Unlike Tandy, who also lost her home in a California fire but had at least some time to pack her valuables, Melissa and her husband had only seconds; they gathered their cats, manually opened the garage doors, jumped into their cars, and drove toward the ocean.

Before reaching the ocean, Melissa found a country road and pulled off, taking twenty minutes to collect herself. She had no radio and no idea that their entire neighborhood and county were on fire; twenty thousand acres would be destroyed within the next twelve hours. Two days later she learned that her home had burned to the ground, and three weeks later she visited her "ash pile." Melissa told me that she felt "numb and grateful to be alive." She continued, "I felt not sad, but stunned. Even seeing the ashes, I felt gratitude. When you look at what's really important, it's the people, not the things. You never know what's around the corner."

Tragedy does not have to precede gratitude; it can be practiced in small, minuscule ways throughout our days. Beverly, a forty-year-old nurse with an easy smile and caring manner who works with psychiatric patients at an outpatient clinic in Louisiana, seemed to have all of the time in the world as we sat together one sunny summer afternoon at a picnic table in her wooded, buggy backyard. When it comes to work, Beverly describes her Purpose as being a compassionate health care worker for her patients. She tries every day to be present and show gratitude to her patients, which she believes is what they need more than anything else. She attributes what she calls her "gift of presence" to what she has learned through her work. Beverly sets aside time each evening after work to handwrite a thank-you note to all of the day's patients. She was especially touched one day when she received a response from one of her patients that read, *Thanks for the card. It means so much. I sleep with it.* Beverly provides just one example of how Presence, Purpose, and gratitude come together to contribute to our own well-being as well as that of others.

Believe it or not, if you write a letter of gratitude, even if you never send it, you can enjoy the mental health benefits of experiencing gratitude. In one study, a test group of psychotherapy clients was instructed to write a letter of gratitude to another person each week for three weeks, a second group was asked to write about their deepest thoughts and feelings regarding negative experiences, and a third did no writing at all. The researchers told the participants in the first group who were assigned to write gratitude letters that they weren't required to send them. Those who wrote gratitude letters reported significantly better mental health four weeks and twelve weeks after the writing exercise ended. Only 23 percent ended up sending the letters, but even those who didn't send their letters enjoyed the mental health benefits of experiencing gratitude nonetheless.

WHAT YOU APPRECIATE APPRECIATES

Cultural Messages and Expectations

When it comes to finding and having Purpose in life, it's essential to distinguish our own values and goals from the cultural messages and expectations of our families and communities, as ultimately the only sense of meaning that matters is what matters to each one of us. This isn't easy. And we cannot do this without Presence. We need to check in with who we are and what's meaningful for us to make sure that the compass we follow is our own, no one else's.

Why do many of us who work in fields such as teaching, nursing, or social work readily diminish our life's work even when we are leading or have led purposeful lives? One reason is that it can be challenging to find or fully appreciate our Purpose when it doesn't "match up" to society's definitions of success—often viewed through the filters of earning at a specified salary level, living in a certain neighborhood, or working within a given industry. It's easy to internalize these beliefs and in turn devalue our own life's Purpose.

Taylor is an earnest, no-nonsense woman who is about to retire from a twenty-five-year career as a speech therapist in the Chicago public school system. When I asked her about her work, she said apologetically, "I haven't had a big, big career and didn't make so much money, but my career was meaningful. My Purpose was to improve the lives of kids' and their families, and I was able to do that. People were depending on me." Toward the end of our interview, Taylor added, "I feel not as valued by myself, and I know that's my issue." We have already talked about the myths, such as "I'm not good enough," that can continue to have a hold on many of us for our entire lives, and Taylor is no exception. Even beliefs we've accepted as our truths may not actually reflect our values—maybe it's a script, or a set of unexamined expectations, that society has prescribed and we've internalized. With that in mind, it's helpful to focus more on how we see ourselves and less on what others impose on us, so that we can live more consistently with our own life's Purpose.

Dr. Pamela McCauley, an engineering professor of more than twenty-five years, is among the 5 percent of African American women who make up the approximately 25 percent of women in science, technology, engineering, and math (STEM). McCauley has made it her life's Purpose to encourage women to enter and stay in STEM. She has spoken to over a million high school students, reminding them: "There is an awesome innovator in you," "STEM is fun, and for you," "You are good enough," and "You can do this." During our interview, McCauley lamented that women can give their best work on par with their male counterparts and still have their work devalued and marginalized. Her words reminded me of a story from my first week as a junior associate at a large law firm in Los Angeles. The opposing counsel on one of my cases called my supervising partner to complain that I was practicing law without a license. It never occurred to him that I was an attorney. I later learned that he was just one year out of law school.

McCauley emphasized how important it is for women to realize that the resistance in STEM is not personal but rather reflects overarching negative cultural attitudes toward women. She herself encountered many personal challenges and adversities that could have halted her entrance into engineering. She was the first in her family to go to college, with limited financial resources and enormous self-doubt. She also had a baby while she was a sophomore in high school, and was a single parent. Against these odds, McCauley ultimately made her way to college and graduate school in engineering. Her parents, the "difference makers," as she calls them, were key to her success.

McCauley recalls a campus survey conducted during her time at MIT, which showed that when women dropped below a certain GPA, they felt they were not good enough and dropped their STEM majors; in contrast, their male counterparts with much lower GPAs chose to remain in STEM. Similarly, studies show that women may be reluctant to apply for jobs requiring some skills that they may not have, and they are more likely to apply only when they're 100 percent qualified, while men are much more likely to apply for the same jobs even if they lack the required skills.

Not Only Leaving but Living Our Legacy

We've discussed how the various domains of our lives may each have their own Purpose, and that finding our Purpose(s) is not one and done but rather a dynamic process. Compared with generations before us, most of us will enjoy an extra twenty years of good health, which means more time than ever before in our human history to pursue our Purpose(s). A thirty- to fifty-year-old woman in the United States today, for example, is expected to live to age eighty-five or eighty-six. These extra years can mean encore careers and multiple pursuits for most of us. And many of us will be able to shift our focus from acquiring—as in family, career, and home—to what psychologist Erik Erikson called *generativity*: beginning to invest outward to the next generation, our community, or a cause. With longer health spans we have more time and energy to not only leave a legacy, but *live* one.

How do we live our legacy? Volunteering can provide a way of living with Purpose and living our legacy. Research suggests that volunteering slows the cognitive decline of aging; individuals who volunteer one hundred hours a year score, on average, about 6 percent higher in cognitive testing than those who don't. It turns out, however, that not all volunteering has the same effect on our well-being: *Why* and *how* we volunteer is important. First, the *why*. Research suggests that volunteering for unselfish reasons, such as feeling "it's good to help others as much as I can," correlates with a longer life span than volunteering out of selfish reasons, such as "it's a great escape from my miseries." Volunteering for the right reasons cuts our risk of death by 60 percent, while volunteering for selfish reasons keeps our mortality rate at approximately the same percentage as for those who did not volunteer at all.

Now for the *how* of volunteering. A greater sense of Purpose can come from volunteering services that are in our area of expertise, and honing skills we've developed over time. This means applying our skills to new environments, which can allow for more personal growth. Any volunteer work that you find personally meaningful—whether or not it's in an area you are familiar with—can provide a sense of Purpose.

Our Purpose drives us as we work to make a difference in the world. So-called generative adults are dedicated to their work, parenting, and mentoring; they desire to leave a legacy behind and are concerned with the well-being of future generations. Research confirms that generative people are healthier and more content than other adults.

Purpose in Brief

Purpose arises out of what matters most to us, what's personally meaningful and in turn provides meaning to our lives. It's rooted in our most treasured, valued goals and gives us direction. Paradoxically, tireless and often thankless work in support of our Purpose, with little concern for personal gain, is a research-supported path to happiness, unlike the pursuit of happiness for its own sake. Purpose also adds resilience to our lives, providing us with joy in good times and resilience in hard times.

SIFT Practice for Purpose

On page 127 is a quick check-in practice you can do in just one minute that can be immensely helpful. Those of you familiar with Dan Siegel's work may know that he appreciates acronyms, one of which is SIFT, whereby we can pause, sift through our mind, and become aware of our sensations, images, feelings, and thoughts. See if by just taking this quick break you will be able to become aware of and better manage whatever is going on. By noticing and sometimes naming what is happening as it is happening, like a wave of emotion or bodily sensation, a challenging experience can be managed with more clarity and calm.

The SIFT practice is also a good way to assist us in finding and sustaining our Purpose by getting us in touch with what's personally meaningful for us. So when you have a few minutes, you may pay attention to what sensations, images, feelings, or thoughts may arise while exploring what's meaningful to you. That's how you can SIFT your mind, for example, to explore Purpose in your life.

Purpose

central,
self-organizing
aim

based on
valued goals

providing
direction

and a sense
of meaning

SIFT PRACTICE FOR PURPOSE

* Get into a comfortable, yet dignified, position with eyes closed, or gaze averted. Take your time to feel settled.

* Bring to mind something that has personal meaning for you. Something that is central to your identity and that energizes you. Remember, it need not be grand or global, but it motivates you to do something that will have an impact beyond yourself.

* Now SIFT your mind by focusing your attention in the following sequence:

  Sensations: What bodily sensations are arising, such as a feeling in your gut, heart, or muscles? In your limbs, trunk, or face?

  Images: What auditory or visual images are arising?

  Feelings: What emotions are present, such as fear, sadness, gratitude, joy, or awe?

  Thoughts: What thoughts come to mind?

* Notice what comes up for you as you SIFT your mind.

* Repeat as needed anytime you are trying to find or sustain your Purpose.

3-Minute Breathing Space

The next time negative emotions get a grip on you, and you find yourself either resisting or entertaining them, try this quick practice.

Make the 3-Minute Breathing Space your first response, your go-to whenever you become aware of being preoccupied, confused, or caught up in a negative thought safari about the past or future. It's an effective way to stop negative emotions in their tracks. Remember, the lifetime of any emotion, including an unpleasant one, is short-lived—perhaps just ninety seconds—unless we try to push it away or engage with it.

And of course, it's beneficial for us to take a 3-Minute Breather any time, not just during our most challenging moments, so that a state of mindful awareness can become a trait, as we've discussed. Below is the 3-Minute-Breathing Space developed by Teasdale, Williams, and Segal who consider this the single most important practice in their entire mindfulness program.

THE 3-MINUTE BREATHING SPACE

- *Become aware.* Sit up comfortably, yet dignified. Close your eyes, or avert your gaze. Take a long inhale and exhale. Ask yourself: What am I experiencing right now? What feelings, thoughts, or bodily sensations? Wait patiently for the answers. Label whatever comes up, even unwanted and unpleasant feelings, thoughts, or sensations. Allow space for anything that arises in your awareness.

- *Gather your full attention to your breath.* Use your breath as an anchor to the present moment. Notice each inhalation and exhalation. Follow each breath, one after the other. Tune into the stillness that's always there, just beneath the surface of your thoughts.

* *Expand your awareness.* Sense the field of awareness around you expanding. Notice your posture, your facial muscles, your hands. Soften any tension. With this open awareness, connect with your whole being, encompassing all that is you in this present moment, the only moment we ever have.

PART 3

Presence and Pivoting

Don't ever make decisions based on fear. Make
decisions based on hope and possibility.
—MICHELLE OBAMA

IF YOU ARE LIKE MOST OF US, you've had plenty of experience with roles—personal or professional—that unexpectedly take over your entire life, whether for days, months, or even years. That's where the second P—Pivoting—comes in. So many roles translate to frequent Pivoting, or turning from one thing to the next, as we keep up with our varying responsibilities, from enrolling our children in a new school, to switching jobs, to helping an elderly parent move into a safer home. And if your life is anything like mine, no two days are the same and you find yourself Pivoting among various roles throughout your day.

I asked in my interviews, "What roles are you playing right now in your life?" Here's a sampling of the responses—*all on top of our family, friend, and work roles*:

mentor,

mentee,

wingman,

simplifier,

connector,

confidante,

go-to person,

support system,

reluctant leader,

caregiver for many,

community builder,

steward of the earth,

cohesiveness captain,

mediator for my siblings,

keeper of the household,

chauffeur for my children, and

anything that nobody else is filling.

I'm sure you can add another role or two of your own. Just pause for a moment right now and think about the roles you play. I know. You just slowed down long enough to read or listen to a book for a few minutes, and here I am asking you to do something. Once you make your mental list of the many roles you play, just stay with that for a moment and appreciate yourself for all that you are managing each day. We don't usually take time to do this. If you are like most of us, you probably more readily appreciate and show gratitude to friends, family, and work colleagues than to yourself. We are usually last on our long to-do lists.

What does playing all of these roles mean for us? It means early mornings and late nights—without regard for time zones—and with a second shift from eight to midnight for "catching up" with work that we couldn't get to during the day, such as making overseas conference calls or packing lunches for the next day. It means more and higher hurdles for women. The paradigms for what our roles require of us easily add up to more than 100 percent of our energy and ourselves, whether it's working, parenting, caregiving, or inhabiting any of the other roles we play.

My favorite story about the roles women play is one with which you may be familiar. Indra Nooyi, former chair and CEO of PepsiCo, was working late one night (she was known for working twenty hours a day, often seven days a week) when she received a call from the then chairman and chief executive of PepsiCo informing her that she was going to be named president of the company and placed on its board of directors. She left work to tell her family and upon arriving home, her mother immediately told her to go back out and buy milk for the morning. She did, and when she returned, she banged the milk on the counter and told her mother that she had just been named president and placed on the board of a large company. Her mother retorted, "*When you enter this house you're the wife, you're the daughter, you're the daughter-in-law, you're the mother. You're all of that. So, leave that damned crown in the garage*" (italics mine). When asked if she felt she made a good role model for other women, Nooyi answered, "Probably not." And years earlier, she had stated, "I don't think women can have it all. . . . We pretend we have it all."

What Is Pivoting?

Pivoting has origins in Old French and dates back to 1605–1615. The noun *pivot* means "any thing or person upon which we depend vitally," as in a rock or an anchor. The anchor is a key feature of Pivoting, just as in basketball when we keep one foot anchored while passing the ball, and the person whom we are depending upon is ourselves. We're all likely familiar with the day-to-day Pivoting that allows us to meet the ever-evolving demands of our work, family, and friends—you'll recall the long list of roles at the beginning of Part 3. Examples include making adjustments in your schedule so that you can be more available to your adolescent daughter who needs more supervision now and covering for a coworker who is on a leave of absence. There's also "crisis Pivoting" that's required when emergencies arise and demand our full, immediate attention—such as a serious illness, unexpected loss of a job, or the death of a loved one. When these life events occur, we drop everything to deal with them.

While crisis is a great motivator for us when it comes to decision making and change, the topic of this part is what I call "proactive Pivoting" for when we are not in crisis mode. When we are curious, engaged, and motivated in our professional and personal lives, we often hit plateaus or find that our interests change. With change as the only constant in our lives, one of our most important tools for our resilience and well-being is proactive Pivoting. We've all likely been in relationships or jobs that "look good from the outside" or "perfect on paper," only to find that at some point, they are no longer serving us well. With Presence we can become aware sooner rather than later of when it may be time for proactive Pivoting. Waiting too long to make changes and finding ourselves near or in a crisis requiring change—whether it's weeks, months, or even years—often means fewer options and a shorter time frame.

Maybe you're beginning to feel burned out, you're feeling trapped in a relationship, or you have that nagging feeling that has you wondering what else might be out there for you, either professionally or personally. We can also consider proactive Pivoting when a change may be needed in order to live consistently with our life's Purpose. It's a methodical approach for navigating change on our terms. Or maybe it's time to pursue a dream deferred for too long as life got in the way, and now's the time for a career change, a travel adventure, or more education. The beauty of Pivoting is that it empowers us to be responsive to life's twists and turns at any point in our lives. It can get us unstuck.

It's not easy to change course or start over, whether that means switching jobs, reassessing a relationship, or considering some other major life change. One thing to keep in mind, whether or not we end up Pivoting, is this: *It can feel freeing to simply know that Pivoting is available to us, even if we choose in the end to not make any change at this time.* It also can be freeing to know that if we make a change and it doesn't work out, we can make another change. And sometimes what we need in the moment is an internal change, a reframe, rather than an external change.

We may tend to associate Pivoting with the greater flexibility or mobility we enjoy in our twenties, thirties, forties, and even fifties, but the fact is that Pivoting is available throughout our entire lives, even into our nineties and beyond! Even after retiring, many of us will find new challenges, take classes, or pursue passions that have been long dormant. All of this means more Pivoting with new directions, from assuming new family roles, to volunteering, to starting a new career.

My mom, Elizabeth, had lived in southern Wisconsin all of her life—for eighty-five years—when she decided to move closer to one of her four children. Since we each live in a different state, Mom could choose among New Jersey, Texas, Colorado, and California. She ultimately chose Texas to be near my sister and brother-in-law. Within the span of about six weeks of making her decision to move, she sold her house and car, gave away a lifetime of personal belongings, packed up over seventy-five boxes, and lovingly put Molly, a bright-eyed shih-poo in a plush carrier and off they went to Texas. What prompted my mom's move at this point in time? Mom is a very practical person and wanted to get settled in a new community while she is still in great health. Not uncommonly, Pivoting in one's eighties can be more crisis Pivoting, as when a medical or legal emergency arises. I admire my mom's proactive Pivoting, and the fact that she acted at a time when she had many alternatives. She was in the driver's seat and took full advantage of that. Proactive Pivoting often means more options.

Proactive Pivoting does usually take planning ahead. Colleen is in her early forties and has worked mostly happily at the Government Office of Accounting as an analyst for more than seven years. When I described Pivoting to her, she said, "Pivoting, no problem! I can adjust readily to anything. What I struggle with is that I don't fully prepare for change." Colleen likened making changes in her life to throwing a ball without first lining up the toss, and then, once she has thrown it, finding herself futilely trying to guide the ball with hand motions. She wishes that she could take time to prepare. To the extent that we can take our time and be thoughtful about our next move, we can avoid further course correction. With Pivoting, the first step is Presence—knowing what the situation is and what our own intentions are. We all have our challenges when it comes to Pivoting, including fear of failure and resistance to change, which we will be discussing in the following sections.

Pivoting

Setting Your Anchor

We've talked about knowing our own stories and the importance of identifying which expectations arise from inside us, rather than from outside us. Pivoting can be especially challenging when we realize that, because of family or cultural expectations, we have made certain choices—perhaps years earlier—that we were never truly aligned with. Mahnoor, in her late thirties, who talks fast and moves even faster, had worked for a decade at a Big Four accounting firm when she decided to leave her profession. She never liked accounting, but she was skilled at it, and with familial pressure and the fact that it's the most honored profession in her native Pakistan, she found herself working as an accountant. Mahnoor finally had the courage to leave her secure position and has just been accepted to law school. She has no idea how she will tell her parents, and they will surely consider it a "step down," but Mahnoor is comfortable with her decision and is looking forward to preparing for her new career as a lawyer.

Pivoting in a work situation also often requires that we figure out how our experience and abilities can be reconfigured in a way that better meets our current needs and will be more rewarding for us. It may mean moving in a new but related direction. Remember, we don't need to abandon our work experience, skills, talent, and resources; rather, they constitute our anchor and can be relied on and often repurposed.

Stacy, an articulate, thoughtful, and joyful single mom of two young children, worked as a newspaper editor for fifteen years and treasured the investigative and writing responsibilities of her work. Once she decided to pursue her lifelong dream of working in radio, it was important to her to be able to continue using her current skill set. And indeed upon making the switch to radio, she found that the investigative, analytical, and writing skills from her editing days were very useful in honing her radio skills. With Pivoting, we aren't starting from scratch. Stacy took it one step at a time—no fast moves. She implemented a plan that involved devoting an hour or two daily to her impending Pivoting, uncertain how much time she would need to make the change. For big moves such as Stacey's, it's worth taking the time to intentionally move forward, little by little.

One of the beautiful features of Pivoting is that it's not a solo operation; you always have the support of your network, including former colleagues, friends, mentors, and *friendtors* (people whom you call friends but who also wear the mentor hat professionally). Before, during, and after Pivoting, we are always anchored within our personal and professional networks, our greatest resource when it comes to Pivoting.

Assessing What's Working Well

When it comes to Pivoting, we sometimes overlook what's going well, since our survival-based brain tends to focus our mind's attention first and foremost on the negative, as many of us have experienced. Rich Fernandez, CEO of Search Inside Yourself Leadership Institute (SIYLI) introduced me to the "3 Ws" a few years ago and I've been applying it ever since in both my professional and personal life. In our offices, we start our meetings by sharing what went well—the "3 Ws"—and what our role was in it. Inevitably, we do get around to discussing what didn't go so well, but having the foundation of the 3 Ws allows us to start at a solid, positive place and makes all of us more receptive to considering how we might make things work more smoothly next time. In full disclosure, we technically start our meetings with a two-minute meditation!

When preparing to change jobs it can help to ask questions such as "What parts of my work do I most enjoy?," "What skills am I using in this position that I'd want to continue using?," and "What's working well for me right now?" The answers to these questions provide the non-negotiables—the things we don't want to give up in our next position. Obviously, these are questions that can't be answered quickly, but they do prompt us to get present with what *is*, and then look at how closely aligned, or not, our work is with our Purpose. Before making your move is the ideal time to ask and start to answer these questions.

Ezgi is an ambitious, gregarious, forty-one-year-old woman, one of the three women I mentioned earlier whom I interviewed in Istanbul. Ezgi had risen quickly and steadily over the past fifteen years in hospitality, loving her career path. Recent terror attacks in Turkey had taken their toll on the hotel industry, so she decided it was time to find a new industry, sooner rather than later. Ezgi now uses her management skills in a completely different environment—a hospital. She wasn't starting over, but rather, she found that the management skills she learned in the hotel industry translated well to a hospital environment. Ezgi is more fulfilled in her new career than ever before, feeling grateful that she had the time to explore various options and land a position that involves so many of the skills she has always enjoyed using. And as mentioned in Part 2 on Purpose, she and her two cohorts at the hospital in Istanbul all have also found their work meaningful at the hospital and very much aligned with their Purposes.

Having the Conversation

Sometimes we overlook the obvious. It's always good to "look before you leap," as in look around you and see if there's an option or a change that you can make short of ending a longtime friendship or marriage, quitting the parent board you've enjoyed serving on for three years, or changing jobs; perhaps an adjustment can be made within the relationship or organization. Sometimes having the conversation—the kind of "tough conversation" that we all dread and would often do almost anything to avoid—can make a difference. That's likely why, believe it or not, there may be options in front of us that go untapped because we don't even consider it—we just don't think of it.

Evan is a thirty-one-year-old environmental scientist and self-proclaimed "protector of our planet" who has worked as a site manager for a vertical-farming company in Chicago over the past four years. When we first started talking about her work, she said that she was ready to resign, as she no longer found managing the crews and day-to-day operations rewarding or meaningful (there's our friend Purpose again). She knew of several other vertical-farming firms in her area, so she already had begun reaching out to them. As we talked, however, she realized that her company has a division that does exactly what she would like to do: grant writing and research on environmental management. So Evan set up a meeting with her supervisor to talk about the prospect of her transferring to a different division. Just a few weeks later, she was transferred and she is once again excited to go to work every day.

Sky Jarrett, a self-proclaimed "recovering, overachieving perfectionist" and former management consultant at Accenture who was instrumental in building its meditation program for over four hundred thousand employees, was rising rapidly up the ranks of the company. By all appearances, her advancement and increased responsibilities signified success, but one day it became crystal clear to Jarrett that she was falling short in other areas of her life. Jarrett's pregnant sister called one morning to let her know that she expected to go into labor that day, to which Jarrett replied, "Are you sure?" Jarrett was so busy at work that she couldn't fathom taking the time to go to the hospital for her niece's birth if it wasn't really going to happen that day.

Some of you may be thinking, "That's unbelievable," while others may be thinking, "Yes, that sounds just like something I would say." In the end, Jarrett decided to go to the hospital and her niece was indeed born that day; only later did she realize how unhealthy her thinking was. Jarrett had been under tremendous pressure at work and in her personal life over the past year; both her cousin and best friend had passed away unexpectedly, and she had been robbed at gunpoint, contracted Lyme's disease, and gone to the emergency room because of a panic attack that she was convinced would end her life. She said, "The only thing that grounded me when all of these things were happening was my meditation practice. I always knew that through it all, I had my breath and my practice."

This accumulation of so many stressors, plus the phone call from her sister about her niece's birth, prompted Jarrett to question the life she was leading. She considers her niece's birth a wake-up call, and, in hindsight, she can't believe she even hesitated to go to the hospital. Ultimately, it didn't work out for Jarrett to stay at Accenture so she transitioned out of her high-powered position and started her own coaching and consulting company which helps people overcome barriers through mindfulness practices.

LIVE
A LIFE
YOU CAN LIVE WITH

Fear of Failure

Our negative brains can easily conjure up all kinds of dreaded scenarios about what may happen to us, especially when we are contemplating changes in our lives. Our fear of making a mistake and failing, for example, can be daunting and paralyzing when it comes to Pivoting. When I asked Stacy, the former newspaper editor who moved to radio, what her biggest hurdle in her Pivoting has been, she replied, "Hands down, it's been fear of failure." I recalled that during our first interview, Stacy told me her plan in confidence, afraid to even mention it to anyone just in case it didn't work out.

We resist change, fear failure, and on top of that, before we have even taken the first step of Pivoting, we may project ourselves into the future and start to dread telling family and friends things didn't work out, announcing to our work colleagues we are leaving, downsizing, moving home with our parents, being unemployed, or becoming unable to support ourselves and our families. Sound familiar? We also don't like giving up as that in and of itself is sometimes seen as failure.

While she was "on the cusp" of Pivoting, Stacy said that she had to be "really brave." At age forty-five, she felt she couldn't make a big switch; she didn't want to leave her job until she had the next one lined up. To overcome her fear of failure and "boost her confidence," she needed to "think or act like a man and charge ahead." When I asked her what that meant, she explained that men often go forward with much less expertise but far more confidence than women. I'm reminded of the classic story about breastfeeding. The following question was posed in a room of several men and women: "Who is an expert in breastfeeding?" Only one person raised his hand: a man who explained that he had watched his wife breastfeed for three months. The women in the crowd, some mothers with breastfeeding experience, didn't consider themselves experts.

Before moving on, let's spend a moment on what is *not* failure, whether in personal or professional settings. We've all been rejected, felt uncertain, and tried things that didn't work out the way we wished or thought they would. I hope that you wouldn't consider any one of these to be a sign of failure. These are feelings and experiences familiar to all of us, inherent parts of being human. A helpful reframe for failure could be: The real failure is in never trying. Failure can provide opportunities for growth, which we'll be talking about in a later section.

Sometimes, fear of failure even causes some of us to create a backup career. Samantha, an ambitious, lively twenty-eight-year-old with wisdom beyond her years, learned as a teenager that she had to make a living and find her own way in the world. Her family was generally distracted with financial and personal challenges of their own, so they were mostly unavailable to her. Samantha finished graduate school with a degree in family therapy and then began a private practice as a therapist and had a baking business on the side. When I asked her about her dual career choice, she explained that her fear of failure forced her to have a backup career to increase her odds for success. Recently, thanks to her meditation practice and what she calls the "power of Presence," she has realized that taking on two careers was due to her fear of failing in her chosen career as a family therapist. Now, Samantha only bakes for fun.

Yogi Berra said it best: "We made too many wrong mistakes." (This is the last Yogi Berra quote!)

Resisting Change

We've been talking about how our fear of failure can inhibit Pivoting and keep us in situations longer than may be optimal for us. What else can get in our way when it comes to Pivoting? We are creatures of habit; we like our routines and familiar surroundings. We tend to resist change. Our brain likes certainty because it helps us survive. Pivoting requires a mindset that is willing to move from the familiar to the unfamiliar, from the predictable to the unpredictable, and from the known to the unknown. That takes courage. Courage isn't the absence of fear; it's moving forward in a thoughtful way even in the face of fear. Pivoting requires getting comfortable with a variety of "what ifs," which isn't easy because our brains prefer certainty. I noticed the following inscription of the words of artist Kameelah Janan Rasheed in the rotunda of the Brooklyn Public Library, just as I was working on this section: "having abandoned the flimsy fantasy of certainty, i decided to wander."

Also in times of proactive Pivoting, whether in our careers or relationships, our brains reason that even though we may find a better situation, we are "happy enough," and the familiar, predictable, and certain often win out. In the weeks leading up to Stacy's resignation from her editing job, for example, she was "trying to be OK with the tension," and felt herself both "resisting the change and leaving the familiar, on the one hand, and being deeply motivated to make the move, on the other hand."

Another challenge when it comes to Pivoting is a phenomenon researchers call *neural loss aversion*. Studies show that we would prefer to avoid losing something rather than gain something else even if it's of equal or greater value. Building on the work of psychologists Amos Tversky and Daniel Kahneman from the late 1970s, Russell Poldrack found that the reactions in our brains were stronger in response to possible losses than to gains. This means that most of us need to know that what we may gain is worth at least twice as much as what we fear losing.

Sometimes a no longer tolerable situation can provide the strength for Pivoting in the face of uncertainty. Priyanka is in her mid-forties and has worked for fifteen years, mostly happily, as a buyer for a major clothing manufacturer. She enjoys the fashion industry, but the pressure of her company's increasingly unrealistic production targets over the past two years, along with constant international travel and 24/7 connectivity, caused her to leave her job, uncertain of what her next step would be. As she put it: "I just knew that staying was not sustainable." Priyanka also wasn't afraid to resign because she's confident she can build her own consulting business from the contacts she has made over the past fifteen years.

Pause here for a moment to consider how these challenges may have gotten in your way when trying to make a change that you knew you had to make. Presence enables us to be aware of our brain's preferences so that we can more easily pave the way for proactive Pivoting.

Growth versus Fixed Mindsets

Pivoting works optimally when we have what psychologist Carol Dweck calls a *growth mindset*. Having a growth mindset means being open and becoming comfortable with change and the uncertain: "Nothing ventured, nothing gained." The hallmark of what Dweck calls the *fixed mindset*, on the other hand, is "Nothing ventured, nothing lost." A fixed mindset holds us back and sometimes keeps us from the unfamiliar, or something that could actually be a very positive growth experience for us. Dweck asserts that rigid, limited thinking benefits no one. The good news is that a fixed mindset can be reoriented to a growth mindset when we decide to embrace challenges as new opportunities to grow and learn.

There's a story attributed to naval officer Frank Koch that illustrates the dangers of a fixed mindset, and the importance of being open. A battleship had been at sea under severe weather conditions for several days. One night, the lookout saw a light in the distance and reported it to the captain. The captain noticed that the light was getting brighter and was not veering to the left or right, which meant the ships were headed straight toward each other. The captain ordered a signal to be given to the other ship, advising it to change course. The response was, "You change course." After several increasingly heated exchanges, the captain instructed his signalman to send back a final message: "I am a battleship. Change course twenty degrees east right now!" Back came the response: "I am a lighthouse."

Here's an example of how a growth mindset can support us in our careers. Laura, an enthusiastic, good-humored, thirty-five-year-old graphic artist with two young children, had spent over seven years working for a large corporation and figured out early in her career that one day she would start her own company, and she did. When I asked how she came to this so early on, Laura said that she had always found meaning in her life beyond her work. She was from a large family, wanted to have her own family one day, and had other interests on the side, including set design. She knew that she'd need more flexibility and freedom than any corporate job could offer her.

With every opportunity she had along the way, she examined it through the lens of "What can this job teach me?" and "How could I consult on this job someday?" She never burned a bridge and methodically built up her contacts so that she could jump-start her own business at the right time. Laura had no idea what it would be like to take the plunge and start her own business. She appreciated the infrastructure of the large corporations she had worked for, and had to muster the courage to handle the uncertainty and unknowns involved in pursuing an independent venture. Nonetheless, she was up to the challenge and welcomed the new experiences and opportunities that come along with starting a business, providing her own tech support, HR, marketing, sales, and business promotion, and of course being her company's graphic artist, all in one.

Now five years into running her own business, Laura admits that her schedule is very hectic, and she's busier than she has ever been. She works out of a home office in her backyard, so breaks during her workday consist of visiting her young daughter, just twenty-five feet away. She always takes a couple of breaths as she walks that short distance in order to make the transition from work to being present for her daughter. This is a beautiful example of an informal mindfulness practice that is making a big difference in how Laura can transition from work to her family. Laura feels that she has two full-time jobs, and she does. However, she wouldn't change a thing—except perhaps to add another six hours to her waking hours! When it comes to balance, she says that as long as she feels content with her choices—and she is—then she is happy.

An essential part of having a growth mindset is being comfortable with the uncomfortable and Pivoting even when we don't know what's next. Perhaps we'll find a situation that we never could have imagined, but that often turns out to be a great fit for us. With Pivoting, we can let everything—even unexpected but necessary change—be our teacher.

Empowered, Not Perfect Decisions

Decision making precedes Pivoting. Sometimes we may have so many choices that we get paralyzed, and other times we convince ourselves that somehow there is a perfect decision. However, no perfect decisions exist. Why? Often the very reason there's a decision before us is that there are two paths, or more, each with its own pros and cons, both known and unknown. Perhaps you're feeling stuck, that your decision is "forever," which only serves to amplify your fears. It can sometimes feel like there is so much at stake, we simply can't move forward.

Another challenge to our decision making is that we often think it takes our best and deepest thinking. What we often overlook is to ask this simple question: "How do I feel about this decision or change?" One way to answer this question is to follow the simple Visualization Practice for Pivoting found at the end of Part 3. This visualization practice can be useful whenever you are facing a decision: whether to stay in a relationship, change jobs, or transfer your child to a different school. The exercise can put us in touch with the deep feeling as opposed to the deep thinking that is so often our go-to in times of decision making. In addition to thinking about a decision, it's essential to access our feelings by visualizing ourselves in a given situation in order to see more clearly whether or not we are comfortable with it.

THERE IS NO PERFECT DECISION.

Embracing New Roles

At whatever stage of life we are in, no matter our age, most of us have found ourselves looking ahead to a time when we thought life would be easier, simpler, or somehow better. But just when we arrive at that point in time, with change as the only constant, something inevitably changes in our lives, often meaning a new role for us. Maybe it's the birth of a child or grandchild, a family member's health challenge, or a corporate reorganization that lands you in a new location or department. Embracing new roles provides plenty of opportunities for Pivoting with a growth mindset, as we discussed earlier.

Anat has boundless energy, a twinkle in her eye, and speaks faster than anyone I know. I can only catch about 60 percent of what she says; her husband has told me that he would often appreciate subtitles! I immediately sensed that she lives life to the fullest. Anat divides her time among three different cities where her three children and five grandchildren live, while she and her husband live in yet another city. She expected to "feel free" by now at age sixty-five—free to visit her adult children when she wants, to spend time with her husband, and to continue to teach English classes at her local community college. With the arrival of her grandchildren over the past few years, however, Anat admits that she feels anything but free. She feels confused and sometimes overwhelmed by her own expectations of what it means for her to be a grandma, as well as her adult children's expectations of her in this new role.

Anat shared that "as wonderful as it is having grandchildren, it does mean the end of your relationship with your own children, as you have known it." She reminisces on how easy it was before her children had children, when she could just visit them in their respective cities, and then leave knowing that they were launching their careers and building their own lives; she was then free to "do her own thing." That lasted for only three short years. The arrival of spouses and grandchildren "seriously shifted" things for her, and has meant—at least for now—the loss of her freedom to come and go.

Anat said that the birth of her two most recent grandchildren made this the hardest year of her life; she finds it challenging to be available to her daughter, who works full time and hopes that Anat will care for the grandchildren, especially when her husband is out of town. Anat finds herself pulled between being there for her daughter and grandchildren, and at the same time continuing to teach English classes back home. Even with all the effort Anat makes to be with her children and grandchildren, she feels the un-asked question from her children is "Why do you have a life?" Anat isn't ready to give up her teaching, and yet she also realizes that her grandchildren are only young once. Pivoting for Anat has also included applying for a teaching position at a high school in her daughter's community so that part of the year she can live near her grandchildren.

Louise is warm, outgoing, and has a beautiful smile. Perhaps not surprisingly, she is a dentist. Louise's wake-up call came the day she returned home from work and heard her son call her babysitter "Mommy." Shortly after that, he referred to her as "dentist lady." Louise said, "I freaked out and thought to myself, 'This is not working.'" Two weeks later, Louise sold her dental practice and started working part-time in a practice near her home in order to be more available for her son. We don't all have the flexibility to move from full-time to part-time positions as Louise did, nor to change our work situations so quickly, but the point is that new roles will often require Pivoting.

So for those of you who thought, as I did, that in the later stages of our lives things would actually slow down, I have bad news: Things don't seem to slow down at all, and in fact they may accel-erate as we enter new relationships as well as treasure long-standing ones, explore more interests, and welcome new family members. Embracing new roles is constant, whether within our families, workplaces, or other parts of our lives, and will bring both shiny and gritty aspects, all requiring Pivoting. The good news is that with Presence we are in charge of how to embrace our new roles and determine what makes sense in light of an up-to-date version of our Purpose in life.

The Machinery of Life Gets Bulkier

Pivoting often requires gradual, well-planned steps that take time to execute over a few months or even years. Perhaps you wish you could make a change immediately, if not yesterday. Not so fast. A thoughtful, realistic assessment of the upcoming months and further reflection may cause you to realize that you need more time before you can make a major change. Perhaps things are good enough for the near future, even though you recognize that you will need to make a change in the coming months or years. This is also where Pacing comes in, and we'll be talking more about that in Part 4.

When I followed up with Stacy four months after she first told me she was planning to leave her position as a newspaper editor, she said, "There's no huge update, as in my new career isn't totally off the ground," but she had been "working pretty diligently" on it. She said that "it's a step-by-step, methodical process," which has included taking classes in radio, reading books, networking, and meeting with a career coach every two weeks. She reflected that when she was younger she could more easily commit to yearlong classes, but now with her job, mortgage, three kids, household, husband, and family, her "web is more complex and it's slow going. *The machinery of life is bulkier, like a big ship versus a wave runner.*" I love this beautiful metaphor, as big boats do swing slower and have a bigger arch than smaller ones. Stacy noted that other classmates can "dance circles around her" in this new field, but she is deeply committed, nonetheless, to finding ways to "wedge in." I could hear the excitement in her voice as she described what she has been learning in her radio classes.

Two years after I first interviewed Stacy, I had a final follow-up with her. She had left her job as an editor and the day I talked with her marked her one-year anniversary at her new job. But it wasn't the job in radio that she had been preparing for. Stacy had barely begun her work in radio when she received news that her best friend from childhood had leukemia. Three months later, on the day her best friend passed away, Stacy vowed to find work with an organization that is working toward a cure for leukemia. Stacy said she was surprised by how quickly she changed course, but it was so clear to her that this move was the "absolute right thing to do," and aligned with her new Purpose. As Stacy's story shows, our Purpose can continue to change and evolve throughout our lives, and the key is to be open and flexible.

Bigger Commitments = Bigger Challenges Pivoting

From Private Practice to *Judge Judy*

I chose corporate litigation as my specialty in law since it seemed a natural fit, given that I had enjoyed college debate and liked the idea of going to court for cases involving a wide variety of industries and issues. However, I had no idea what being a corporate litigator would mean for the other parts of my life. Additional challenges surfaced as the years went by, as my practice required travel and consisted of primarily Japanese clients, which, due to the International Date Line, meant many vanished weekends.

As I was leaving my office one evening around 9 p.m., on my way home to Dan and Alex, our then-five-year-old son, one of my partners called down the hall, "Another half day?" He was only half kidding. Of course, this shouldn't have been a surprise to me. At a previous firm, the only other female partner took me aside my first week and let me in on her secret to success: She kept a sleeping bag under her desk and advised me to do the same. Not unlike many other large corporate law firms, working late or through the night is a common occurrence. On weekends, it wasn't a question of whether we would be in the office, but when. Our 24/7, global, corporate culture isn't confined to law, tech, retail, consulting, finance, or any other industry: It's pervasive in so many more fields. I'm sure that many of you work beyond full time with nonstop, around-the-clock connectivity and demands.

That being said, I did love the work and if I could have cloned myself, perhaps I would have stayed in the practice I had enjoyed for over twelve years. However, with a young son and lots of international travel on top of long hours in my office, I opted to find a career path that would offer more flexibility. I didn't know exactly what that would be. I just knew that my life was not sustainable as it was and I needed to make a change. After dreading for weeks telling my colleagues that I was leaving the firm, I was met with some surprising—and refreshing—responses, such as "I wish I could leave," "Take me with you," and "I'm planning to resign in six months," especially from those whom I had perceived to be among the most committed. All of that worry and dread for nothing. I left my firm without a tangible plan. My first task was to figure out what I wanted and clarify my Purpose with respect to my family as well as my work.

A few weeks after I left my firm, a colleague called to ask if I would consider working part-time as a production attorney on a brand-new reality TV show to be hosted by a former Manhattan family court judge named Judith Sheindlin. That was great timing, as I was in the midst of Pivoting and had started exploring options (just as I've recommended to you!). The producers weren't sure for how long I might be needed as it was a new show. Nonetheless, I was intrigued by the opportunity to put my legal training to work in a different environment, so the following week I was on my way to the Sunset Gower Studios in Hollywood.

I arrived on the lot, went through security, and entered a dimly lit, chilly, cavernous studio. I carefully made my way over the cords and cables that lined the floor and passed the long table of tempting snacks, beyond the sound room, to the production offices. The first person I met was a producer who asked, "Who are you and who sent you?" When I replied, "Corporate legal," he rolled his eyes and said something like, "Ugh, I had no idea you were coming." Eventually we would become friends and establish a great working relationship, sharing a mutual love for our work on the show as well as for our dogs.

For the next two years, I was the production attorney on the set of the show, which came to be known as *Judge Judy*. I had to be on the set for tape days, which amounted to about six days a month, and of course there was some work associated with the show in between those tape days. Nevertheless, I finally had a schedule that didn't consume the majority of my waking hours. Good-bye, seventy-hour workweeks!

About two months into my new job, my cousin Greg came to visit from Kansas City. When I told him about my new, fun work, he said, "Go and get a real job!" Of course, I knew what he was thinking: that my former full-time position as a corporate litigator in an international law firm was more solid and had more of a future than working on the set of a brand-new reality TV show.

I did think twice about what Greg had said, but in the end, I concluded that Pivoting into the *Judge Judy* position was just the right thing at the right time for me. When I accepted the part-time position with the show, it wasn't the time for me to have the most demanding legal position of my career, as I needed space for another important Purpose, that of being an engaged parent for our two young children.

One stark contrast between the corporate culture on the *Judge Judy* set and the one I had left behind at my law firm was that at my new job, I could bring my whole self to work. Big-firm corporate law practice had meant rarely, if ever, mentioning my children to my all-male corporate partners and finding acceptable excuses for time to attend their doctor's appointments and school performances. I spent two wonderful seasons on the *Judge Judy* set prior to moving to a full-time position as in-house counsel at Spelling Entertainment. On Bring Your Kids to Work day at Spelling, I brought our son, Alex, then age eight, who was most impressed that day not by the flashy movie posters that lined the walls, or the TV in my office, but by the parking space that had my name on it!

Stepping Off the Career Track

It's not easy to step off the career track or to cut back on our hours when we enjoy what we do; however, when family or other priorities make it clear that Pivoting is necessary, that's exactly what we have to do. You may wish that you could clone yourself, as I often did, but of course you can't. It's challenging to even consider not working for a time or working less because we may fear missing the stimulation of our work, a certain lifestyle that having an income supports, and our workplace friends and colleagues. When we are in the trenches, we often can't imagine leaving and we can easily become paralyzed by fears, including fear of the unknown, of boredom, and of isolation. When we enjoy our work, perhaps the most frightening fear of all is that we will never be able to get back on track. For those leaving demanding jobs for more flexibility, the challenge becomes finding rewarding work given our time constraints. This requires— you know what I'm going to say—both Presence and Purpose: Presence to check in with ourselves, and Purpose to look closely at what has meaning for us right now.

Bobby is a thirty-five-year-old mom of a son with special needs, who resigned from her full-time position as a hospital administrator a year ago. Bobby decided that at this point it was important for her to be able to focus on her son full time. When she announced her resignation, her former work colleagues told her that she was making a terrible move and she obviously was not serious about her career. She was saddened but not surprised. She told me she misses the stimulation of her work every single day but has resolved that this decision makes sense for her and is fully aligned with what's most important to her right now. As Bobby puts it: "The right job at the wrong time is the wrong job."

Danielle is articulate, energetic, and exudes confidence; by the end of our interview, I wanted her to run my life. For her, Pivoting meant leaving her high-powered career in finance when her third child was born. That was two years ago and she hasn't worked outside the home since. Danielle and her husband were both excelling in their demanding careers in finance, trying to make it work with two young children and a third on the way. Both of their jobs required extensive overseas travel, and between the two of them, they had spent over 250 nights a year in hotels for three consecutive years. They ultimately concluded that moving full speed ahead with both careers was not sustainable, and so they made the necessary financial adjustments so that they could live on one income and Danielle could stay at home with their children. Part of Pivoting for them included downsizing their home, taking their kids out of private schools, and moving to a neighborhood with a good public school system.

While Danielle is grateful to see her family functioning much better now that there's a full-time parent on site, she does face new challenges. She not only misses the work life she had but is also part of a Facebook group from her graduate school days, where she follows the exciting careers of her former classmates. This makes her feel sad because she misses being in the working world with her colleagues, and also finds staying at home lonely since all of her mom friends are working full time as the primary breadwinners for their families.

Danielle never saw herself Pivoting out of the workplace to be a stay-at-home mom for their three children or thought that she and her husband would have assumed such traditional roles. One more challenge for Danielle has been coming to terms with being a stay-at-home mom. She feared that her mother, a full-time career woman, would judge her. She laments, "I wish my mom had told me I could choose to be a stay-at-home mom, and that would be OK."

Over time, the good news for Danielle has been that in stepping off her career track, she has learned that she doesn't need to keep going for the extra credit, as she has done all of her life up until now. Although she wonders if she'll ever be able to get back on track, she has embraced her traditional role, at least for now, and has taken a long view of her life, what I call Pacing. We'll be talking more about Pacing in Part 4. Meanwhile, Danielle is happy to be using her skills in finance while serving on her local school district board and feeling content overall with her life.

Studies show that part-time moms encounter some of the biggest challenges, since they often feel that they don't have sufficient time for either their jobs or taking care of their children. When they're at work, they may not get assigned the best work because of their part-time status, and when they're at home, they think they should be at work. So it's more challenging to find fulfillment in either role.

Those of us with children need to come to our own resolution of how to handle the ever-present work and motherhood quandary, especially when we have young children. Some of us can't imagine not working, while others, like Danielle, come to embrace being stay-at-home moms. Among the women I interviewed, one of whom returned to work six weeks after her second child was born said, "It's saving my life." Similarly, Barbara told me, "I would have gone mad if I didn't work when they were young." Also, not all of us have flexibility when it comes to fewer hours, and not working is not an option for many of us, for financial or other reasons. Further, we don't have to be parents to encounter these quandaries, as life offers each of us a variety of all-consuming personal or professional endeavors outside of work and parenting.

Getting Back on the Career Track

After taking time off, whether because of medical, caregiving, or any number of other reasons, many women decide to return to their careers, either the one they left or a new one. Reentry into the workplace is challenging, and it's important to not become discouraged while searching for work. Jaime, a low-key, happy-go-lucky forty-year-old social worker with young children, has worked part-time for three years and has been interviewing for full-time jobs over the past six months. She is, in her words, "more than ready" to go back to work full time, but meanwhile she's keeping her part-time job as she searches for her next position.

Not everyone ultimately gets back on track, or chooses to get back on track, even if that was their initial plan. Betty is in her sixties and the proud mom of a son who graduated from college six years ago. She left her career when her son was born, which coincided conveniently with changes at her workplace that made her feel "they owned me, lock, stock, and barrel." Betty looks back and reflects that her career was very rewarding for a long time, but that changed with certain corporate changes. Being a full-time mom started as a break from her demanding career, and Betty had planned all along to figure it out after a few months off and go back to work. While she was raising her son, her mantra was: "I'm going back to work." That was twenty-four years ago.

What happened? How did Betty not get back to her career as she had planned? She explained that over time, fear prevented her from returning to work. She would ask herself, "Maybe I've lost my touch? Am I too old? Will I be on top of my game? Can I be as successful as I was before?" She says, "If I had it to do over, I wish I'd gone back to work sometime along the way when my son was in school."

No matter how long we may have been out of the workforce, resources are increasingly available for those seeking to return to work. Many companies now offer *returnships*, which are similar to traditional internships but help adults who have taken time away from their careers to reenter the workforce. Returnships last anywhere from a few weeks to a few months, offer payment commensurate with level of experience, and provide extra training and mentorship. They are especially attractive as they enable us to explore options within or outside our past work experiences.

Similarly, Apple, Oracle, Intuit, Udemy, GoDaddy, Campbell Soup, and many other companies are part of Path Forward, an organization that offers a program to retrain individuals and reconnect them with the workplace to help them jump-start their careers once again. The program has been successful so far—of those who graduated from Path Forward's program recently, 85 percent had a job within six months of finishing.

There's also a career reentry organization called iRelaunch, which supports forty blue-chip companies in developing, piloting, and publicizing a given company's efforts to hire relaunchers who ultimately may be placed directly into open positions without internships. iRelaunch places 50 to 100 percent of the participants into full-time jobs, depending on the company; 93 percent of its participants are women. As iRelaunch founders Carol Fishman Cohen and Vivian Steir Rabin put it: "There's a changing perception about age, and that's in part because of the whole relaunch movement. *Being an expert in your subject matter is an antidote to ageism. Focus on what you know, not how old you are*" (italics mine).

Other useful programs for those getting back on the career track include the worldwide Lean In Return to Work Circles, where groups meet once a month to discuss their dreams, ideas, and concerns, and ReBoot Career Accelerator for Women (their in-person programs/groups are located in Northern California), which offers various online and in-person training, support, and placement programs to help women land jobs and return to the workplace.

Quests and Adventures

Why quests and adventures? Well, they're a part of Pivoting, too. "Chance favors the prepared mind," and so why not give yourself this additional option just in case your life might lend itself to such an opportunity? A quest is a journey with a specific mission or goal, often requiring great exertion and much travel. It very well may be challenging and something that your family and friends will find puzzling.

Throughout history, women have defied convention to undertake awe-inspiring journeys. In the mid-1700s, Jeanne Baret became the first woman to circumnavigate the globe after joining the world expedition of Admiral Louis-Antoine de Bougainville by disguising herself as a man. Similarly, in the early nineteenth century, British adventurer Lady Hester Stanhope became the first European woman to cross the Syrian desert and visit its ancient capital, Palmyra. After a shipwreck off the coast of Egypt, in which Stanhope lost most of her possessions, she started dressing like a man and did so for the remainder of her life.

Nellie Bly, an American journalist in the late 1800s, set off to beat the fictional record set by Jules Verne's Phileas Fogg in *Around the World in 80 Days*. When she suggested the trip to her editor, he replied that it was a great idea but he'd have to send a man—after all, as a woman, Nellie would need a chaperone and dozens of trunks. Eventually, he gave in to her request, and Nellie didn't even have to dress like a man. Nellie completed her journey in just seventy-two days, landing in New York on January 25, 1890, and paving the way for female reporters to expand their journalistic horizons.

You may be thinking, "Hmm . . . why would I go out on a quest or adventure?" Many of us set out on adventures to "find ourselves." Several years ago, when I was teaching in Japan, a blue aerogram arrived in my mailbox from Debra Crow, a college friend who was teaching in Australia at the same time. She proposed that we purchase round-the-world one-way airline tickets, with unlimited stops as long as we continued in the same direction, and so we did. Three months later we set out from Japan with our backpacks and visited twenty-three countries over the next year.

Whether you are considering Pivoting in response to an external event, such as loss of a job due to downsizing at your company, or an internal sense that it's finally the time for you to do that one thing you have always wanted to do, the point is to be aware of the possibility of pursuing this new challenge. Adventures need not involve uprooting yourself or traveling. Perhaps it's a matter of building something in your own community or discovering what might be available in your own neighborhood.

....

More reliably than anything else on earth, the road will force you to live in the present.

—*GLORIA STEINEM*

Pivoting in Brief

With change as the only constant in our lives, Pivoting offers us a way to make necessary adjustments, while knowing that we still have our relationships, resources, and life experiences to rely on. Whether you're wondering if there is work that would be more meaningful or you have deferred a dream for decades as life got busy, Pivoting provides a way forward. Fear of the unknown and of failure, as well as resistance to change are all challenges we may face when it comes to making changes, small or large, in our personal or professional lives. Pivoting allows us to embrace uncertainty, make empowered decisions, and move beyond the paralysis that can get in our way, knowing all the while that we remain grounded, and of course, can make further changes if need be.

PIVOTING ROAD MAP: NOW IS A GOOD TIME FOR A CHANGE

Stages	Action Items
Setting anchor	Drawing on our resources, skills, and experience Assessing what's working well Having the conversation
Overcoming the hurdles	Fear of failure Resisting change Growth mindset versus fixed mindset Empowered, not perfect decisions
Making the change	Planning ahead Determining the best time

Remember: Pivoting (again) is always an option!

Mini-Meditations Throughout the Day

I'd like to introduce you now to what Sharon Salzberg calls *mini-meditations*. Salzberg reminds us that our day-to-day, ordinary life activities offer opportunities for small bursts of meditation anytime, which are great for shaking off distractions or anxieties and restoring concentration and calm. You pick the place, you pick the time. As Salzberg says, "Anywhere we happen to be breathing, we can be meditating." She suggests we grab a quick centering moment—as little as three breaths is fine.

Perhaps you can try taking three mindful breaths before answering an email, while waiting for your daughter's volleyball game to begin, or while in line for your morning coffee. When in your day can you take a moment or two? Just pick a time that can work for you. Our routines can most likely become our cues for the mini-meditations, so that mindful moments can consistently be built into our day. Salzberg describes the benefits of mini-meditations this way: "These moments of stealth meditation may restore the calm state we achieve in longer practice sessions, and they remind us that the breath is always there as a resource, to center us so we remember what matters."

The following is a mini-meditation that can be used throughout your day, and I invite you to try it soon and see if you notice any difference in how you feel after using it for a few days in a row.

MINI-MEDITATIONS THOUGHOUT THE DAY

- Pick your moments, routinely or leaving them random.

- Keep your eyes open.

- Focus your attention on the sensation of your breath, at the nostrils, chest, or abdomen, whichever is most comfortable for you.

- Follow three breaths, and repeat anytime.

- Enjoy!

~~~~~~~~~~~~~~~~~~~~~~~~~~~~~~~~~~~~~~

Visualization Practice for Pivoting

When it comes to Pivoting and decision making, remember that it starts with Presence and the ability to get out of our thoughts and in direct touch with our feelings. One way to begin to overcome the uncertainty, the fear, and the resistance to change that often go along with making difficult decisions is to try this visualization practice.

VISUALIZATION PRACTICE FOR PIVOTING

Get comfortable and close your eyes or soften your gaze.

Take a few deep breaths, noticing and releasing any tension.

Call to mind the decision you are facing.

Notice what it's like not to have a clear answer.

Notice any areas of tension, any thoughts or feelings about being stuck.

Consider your options and imagine yourself on a main road with different paths off it.

Now choose a path to one of your options—imagine what it would look like to take it.

Notice how you feel as you follow the side path to that option.

How do you feel as you approach the scene? Anxiety, excitement, relief, or—?

Take a deep breath and notice your surroundings.

Can you see yourself in that scene?

How does it feel?

Do you like what you feel and see?

Sit with the scene for a moment.

Now say good-bye to the scene and head back to the main road.

You can come back later.

Notice how you feel as you walk away from the scene.

How do you feel as you approach the main road again? Anxiety, excitement, relief, or—?

Back on the main road again, with its different side paths in front of you, how do you feel?

Take a few deep breaths, and when you're ready, open your eyes.

PART 4

Presence and Pacing

A long view of time can replenish our sense
of ourselves and the world.
—KRISTA TIPPETT

THE THIRD P IS PACING, and I'll be using it here to refer not only
to the speed at which we move through our day-to-day lives, but also to
the importance of taking a long view of our life spans. Pacing also
means leaving space for the unexpected that might arise on a given
day, whether happy or sad events. Sometimes our calendars are so full
that even the news of a dear friend arriving in town without notice
is stressful and can be seen as a disruption in our overscheduled lives.
Often, we try to pack multiple goals and priorities into one given
phase of our lives when in fact it may be preferable to spread them
out over time. Surely, we can't do everything, read everything, and
respond to everything; even if we stayed up all night every night, or
worked tirelessly for months, we still couldn't get it all done.

I know it must seem ironic that suddenly I'm saying, "Now may
not be a good time," when I've been emphasizing being in the
moment, but it is Presence, paired with Purpose and Pacing, that

allows us to see our lives with a wider lens. For example, if your elderly parent is requiring more attention lately, it may not be the time to leave your job and start the small business that you always wanted. Pacing puts a pause in our plans so that we can take a closer look at what our Purpose is and what can realistically get done this week, and over the next several months, or years.

The longer we live, the more interests we discover: "There never seems to be enough time to do the things you want to do, once you find them," as Jim Croce put it. Even with our longer health spans that allow us to pursue more and more of our interests, enjoy more years with our loved ones, and have second and third careers, I imagine that many of us still feel that we don't have enough time. Not everyone is happy with this development of more options for our middle and later years. As one mom of two young children whom I interviewed put it, "Yes, I know all about Pacing—grandparents are not available to babysit anymore because they are so busy!"

IF I COULD LIVE MY LIFE OVER

I'd dare to make more mistakes next time.

I'd relax, I would limber up. I would be sillier than I had been this trip. I would take fewer things seriously. I would take more chances. I would climb more mountains and swim more rivers. I would eat more ice cream and less beans. I would perhaps have more actual troubles, but I'd have fewer imaginary ones.

You see, I'm one of those people who live sensibly and sanely, hour after hour, day after day. Oh, I've had my moments, and if I had to do it over again, I'd have more of them. In fact, I'd try to have nothing else. Just moments, one after another, instead of

living so many years ahead of each day. I've been one of those
people who never go anywhere without a thermometer, a hot
water bottle, a raincoat, and a parachute. If I had to do it again,
I would travel lighter than I have.

If I had my life to live over, I would start barefoot earlier in the spring
and stay that way later in the fall. I would go to more dances. I
would ride more merry-go-rounds. I would pick more daisies.

Nadine Stair
85 years old
Louisville, Kentucky

In Part 4, we'll be discussing how Pacing can, as Nadine Stair
suggests, encourage us to start barefoot earlier in the spring and stay
that way later in the fall.

What Is Pacing?

With origins in Middle English, Old French, and Latin, the term
pacing dates back to 1250–1300. By definition, *pacing* refers to "a
rate of movement," as in at what speed you walk, run, or take in
your life, or "a rate of activity, growth, or tempo," as in making
steady progress. The Latin root of *pacing* is *pandere*, which means
"to spread," and the Greek word for *pacing*, *petannynai*, means "to
spread out," as in taking a long view of our lives.

Amy is a social worker, unflappable with a can-do attitude, and
a mom of school-aged children. After her mother passed away and
she was under pressure at work, Amy went into triage mode when
her ten-year-old son was hospitalized and her father-in-law needed
to be moved to a rehab facility immediately—all within just one

Doing it all, all at once = Unsustainable

week. She asked herself every morning: "What's the most demanding emergency? What can I move down the list with the least drastic consequences?" She explained, "You just use whatever capacity you have to deal, and decide whose need is greatest at the moment. Then the shuffle game begins, knowing that as the day goes on, new things will likely arise to supersede the ones so carefully ordered just hours earlier." She knows what it is to never get to the bottom of a to-do list. For Amy, frequently taking moments for herself as part of the daily mindfulness practice she had cultivated over the past seven years and keeping the long view of her life in mind have been essential.

Doing It All, All at Once

I graduated from law school in the 1980s when the message for women was that "you *can* have it all" and "you can do *anything*." My law school class was 50 percent women at a time when women made up only 10 percent of practicing lawyers; today, women comprise approximately 35 percent of practicing lawyers. "You can do *anything*," for many of us, meant, "you can do *everything*." We thought that if we charged full speed ahead, accelerating toward top careers, seeking (but not always finding) blissful romantic relationships, having children (or not), parenting with the most enlightened methods, finding fun friends, and volunteering in our communities, we would feel successful and fulfilled. But for many of us, trying to do it all, all at once—at least in the way that some of us envisioned it and tried it—was unsustainable.

As Amy Westervelt, journalist and cohost of the *Range* podcast, puts it, "We tell women to lean in . . . I'm leaning so far in I'm falling flat on my face." Westervelt is likely alluding to the controversial debate that surrounded Facebook COO Sheryl Sandberg's first book, *Lean In*, and its proposition that women just need to "lean in" to be successful, including sharing household chores and child care 50/50 with their partners. A couple of years later, after the tragic passing of her husband, Sandberg admitted that *Lean In* did not consider the difficulties that many women face, especially single mothers. In her next book, *Option B*, Sandberg discussed how we can find strength in the midst of tragedy and included an apology: "When I wrote *Lean In*, some people argued that I did not spend enough time writing about the difficulties women face when they don't have a partner. They were right. *I didn't get it.* I didn't get how hard it is to succeed when you are overwhelmed at home."

We frequently have responsibilities that converge at the same time, and we often somehow expect ourselves to take them all on simultaneously and excel at each one. Recall the myths we talked about earlier, such as "I'm not smart enough, efficient enough, or fast enough." If only we could work longer or faster, we could get it all done. These converging obligations can often require much of our attention for long periods of time. For example, in our twenties, thirties, and forties and beyond, our responsibilities may include furthering our education, supporting ourselves and our families financially, selecting and developing our careers, cultivating relationships with a significant other and friends, raising children and adolescents, running a household, and giving back to our communities.

In our fifties, sixties, and seventies and beyond, our responsibilities may include advancing or changing our careers, cultivating and maintaining relationships, furthering our education, mentoring, parenting or advising adult children, grandparenting, caring for aging parents, moving to a new place, dealing with health issues of our own and those of loved ones, and contributing to our communities. Pacing allows us to recognize what stage of life we are in and to adjust the rhythm of our lives, in an effort to be aware that our lives are (hopefully) full of healthy years that will allow us to ultimately live consistently with as many of our life Purposes as possible—just not all, all at once.

The basic question to ask is, "What's realistic for me at this time?" This question is very different from asking what's possible. In other words, just because something might be possible, doesn't mean that it makes sense in our lives at this time. The roles we can maintain simultaneously—and realistically—in any given life chapter depend on several factors, including financial circumstances, familial responsibilities, our own energy levels, the nature of the demands of our careers, and support from family, friends, and our workplaces, to name a few. Realizing that we can't do it all, all at once, does not mean not pursuing something that's important to us, but it may mean not pursuing it right now, or making other adjustments in our commitments.

Fluent

....

I would love to live
Like a river flows,
Carried by the surprise
Of its own unfolding.
—JOHN O'DONOHUE

Life Is Many Marathons and a Series of Sprints

For most of human history, the average worldwide life span was much less than fifty years, while in the United States today, the majority of babies born since 2000 will live to be one hundred years old. As we've discussed, our health spans are also increasing, particularly if we live a healthy lifestyle and are born with a reasonably cooperative body and mind. Extended health spans mean many marathons. And just as in a marathon, life's courses can change, depending on what challenges we may encounter along the way. Our enduring effort is required, and we need to figure out how to set a consistent pace in order to best deal with things as they arise. Imagine taking on a marathon (many of us can only *imagine* a marathon, myself included), whether by walking, running, or wheelchair-racing, and all of the things we might encounter that we didn't anticipate—muscle cramps, wet and cold weather, a slippery, muddy course. What's to be expected is the unexpected—and our life's marathons are no different.

Sequencing is another way of incorporating Pacing in our lives and has traditionally referred to the interruption of a woman's career in order to have and care for children until they reach a given age, which varies widely depending on personal circumstances. Given the large numbers of women who are the sole or main breadwinner in their families, and the exciting career opportunities available to women, this definition is outdated. Sequencing today is less about interrupting or leaving careers and more about modifying them in order to accommodate other demands of our lives, including child-rearing.

Anne-Marie Slaughter spent her career in academia at Princeton, and although her work was demanding, she could set her own schedule most of the time. That was no longer the case when she took a position in Washington, D.C., as the first female director of policy planning at the State Department under Hillary Clinton. She resigned after two years—not only because she didn't want to lose her tenure at Princeton but also because of her conclusion that juggling high-level government work with the needs of two teenage boys was not possible. Slaughter lamented that she frequently gets reactions from women age sixty and older who express disappointment: "Women of my generation have clung to the feminist credo we were raised with, even as our ranks have been steadily thinned by unresolvable tensions between family and career, because we are determined not to drop the flag for the next generation. But when many members of the younger generation have stopped listening on the grounds that glibly repeating 'you can have it all' is simply airbrushing reality, it is time to talk." Slaughter's return to Princeton is a great example of Pacing, as she left a high-powered position that was no longer sustainable due to other priorities and made a change appropriate to her next chapter of life.

Part of Pacing is also recognizing what chapter of life we are in and pursuing the things we may not be able to easily pursue later on.

In my mid-twenties, for example, as I was finishing graduate school at the University of Southern California, I had the opportunity to live and work in Japan as an English teacher, which was neither in the field I had studied nor what I planned to do for the rest of my life. I could not think of a more exciting life chapter at that time. I knew that there would be plenty of time to go to law school (if that was still what I wanted to do) and get going on my "real life" later. When I left for Japan, I thought that I would stay for only a few months, but I ended up staying for three years of sprints and marathons.

Beth, a sixty-five-year-old scientist and divorced mom of adult kids and two grandchildren, was the first woman to major in water chemistry at her college, at a time when most women chose either wildlife management or fisheries; she now works as an environmental health consultant. I sense her confidence immediately, thanks to her clear manner of speaking and unwavering eye contact. Beth has been setting up entire communities of seventy to eighty people in remote oil drilling locations in Alaska for the past thirty years. Each project is a marathon in and of itself, requiring Beth's full attention during the two to six months required for each assignment. Here's how Beth describes it: "From setup to completion, I am and have to be fully aware of what goes on around me. The stakes are high. If we don't bring it in, we don't have it, so I have to be extremely present, focused, methodical, and detail-oriented."

Beth also ran the marathon, familiar to many women, of having children while furthering her education. She has fond memories from graduate school of riding bicycles to campus with her then-husband during the Midwest winters, with their two small children tucked inside their down jackets. Not only was she running a marathon, but she was also sprinting, for example, when she or one of her children was sick or during exam week.

Unlike a marathon, which may include a variable pace with

both walking and running (at least for some of us), a sprint has a relatively short time frame and requires all-out exertion. As in our lives, sometimes we can determine the intensity, but at other times, we encounter circumstances beyond our control, which require us to devote ourselves completely to something. Both marathons and sprints are a part of our lives, and sometimes we are moving simultaneously in and out of both in our work and personal lives.

To Manage

She writes to me—
> *I can't sleep because I'm seventeen*
> *Sometimes I lie awake thinking*
> *I didn't even clean my room yet*
> *And soon I will be twenty-five*
> *And a failure*
> *And when I am fifty—oh!*
> *I write her back*
> *Slowly slow*
> *Clean one drawer*
> *Arrange words on a page*
> *Let them find one another*
> *Find you*
> *Trust they might know something*
> *You aren't living the whole thing*
> *At once*

That's what a minute said to an hour
> *Without me you are nothing*

—NAOMI SHIHAB NYE

Getting Unstuck

What if you have such an overscheduled, complicated life with so many priorities that you feel paralyzed and can't move forward? Part of getting unstuck, especially in times of being overwhelmed, is not only considering what's in furtherance of our Purpose but also identifying our daily, weekly, or monthly priorities, as well as nonpriorities. We can move nonpriorities further down or off our to-do list. Though we try to accomplish seemingly innumerable tasks in a day, *we must first come to terms with the hard reality that everything will neither get done nor done in the way we may prefer.* "Selective neglect" is a useful tool for deciding what we can postpone or let go of; *we can choose to not pay attention to our lowest priorities*, at least not at this time. Only in this way can we continue to ensure that we have the time we need for the valued goals that bring meaning to our lives.

One recent morning in March, I was trying to figure out what I had to do that day without fail. Competing priorities kept popping into my head; I had to revise two contracts for work from earlier in the week that I hadn't gotten to, get back to my niece about her spring break visit, organize our tax records for our accountant, finish reading a book for my book club, call Mom, deliver soup to my sick neighbor, order a wedding gift for a colleague, and read through our holiday cards! Yes, you read that right—it's March and I've just now discovered another pile of holiday cards that I hadn't yet read. (And yes, we still receive paper holiday greetings!) I found myself overwhelmed and paralyzed.

So what did I do? I selectively neglected everything, except calling Mom, delivering soup, and preparing for our accountant. Everything else could wait. What was the process? I had to ask myself, "Are there things that can wait? Are there things that may actually disappear if I wait?" "Is anyone's work being delayed by my not acting on this today?" We often function with such a frenetic take-charge approach that we can easily lose sight of the power of prioritizing our priorities, which can ultimately save time and help us get unstuck when overwhelmed.

Jennifer immediately drew me in with her quick smile and strong voice. Now in her late thirties, she looks back and reflects that during her twenties, she felt she had a larger margin for error for personal and professional development. She says that although she has checked certain boxes, such as education, she feels she needs to get her real career going. She's worried about falling behind in the workforce, finding her life partner, having kids, and deciding on where to settle down. Having so many important life unknowns on her checklist was daunting and overwhelming. Once Jennifer took the long view and realized that her boxes didn't need to be checked all at once, she felt more calm and peaceful.

....

Knowledge is learning something every day.
Wisdom is dropping something every day.

—LAO TZU (PARAPHRASED)

Setting the Pace

Who's in charge of setting the pace? It's you. You're in the driver's seat. I'm talking about our routine, ordinary days where we actually have more control over our pace than we may think. Antonyms of Pacing include scurrying, scampering, skipping, and darting. As you envision yourself on any given day, which pace most often reflects you?

Sandra, CEO of a health care group of 1,500 physicians and mom of two teenagers, describes Pacing this way: "It requires saying no to the firefighting mode. *There are endless things to do.*" She always asks herself, "What will happen if these five things don't get done today? Will the world end?" And the answer is usually no. Sandra also says that when it comes to Pacing, she works hard and plays hard, so during vacations, for example, she disconnects completely, explaining: "In two weeks, not much can change. They won't harm anyone and they won't lose too much money." Sandra said she is OK with a few mistakes and believes her team can learn from their mistakes. Pacing means not only saying no to the firefighting mode, but also saying no more often than many of us are inclined to do. We'll be talking more about saying no later in this part; in fact, it's so important to Pacing that I've devoted an entire section to it.

Another aspect of Pacing is the often counterintuitive act of slowing down, pausing, or even stopping, if only briefly. Why counterintuitive? For many of us, slowing down is the last thing on our mind when we are trying to meet deadlines and get through our demanding days. However, taking breaks can be a powerful source of strength and rejuvenation. It's also important to regularly give ourselves time off—to play, relax, and get away from normal routines. However, some of us may think we are "too busy" to take the vacation time we have. Studies show, for example, that 84 percent of executives have canceled vacations for work. Some of my former law colleagues would boast to Dan during our annual holiday parties that they had not taken a vacation in two or three years, and one colleague even postponed her honeymoon for a year due to her work. Both breaks during our days as well as vacations are important for our well-being. And it turns out that making space *throughout* our day-to-day life is more effective than "saving it all up" for a single two-week vacation.

We've been talking about Pacing during our routine days, but I'd like to include one story about Pacing when we do not have much, if any, control. Major life events, such as accidents and illnesses, whether of loved ones or ourselves, can slow us down and drastically change our world within seconds. Jessica, an avid and experienced bicyclist, was thirty-six when she lost control of her bike on Pacific Coast Highway in Southern California one sunny Saturday morning and had to be airlifted to UCLA. Over the next three years, she learned to walk again and since the accident she has just been putting her life "*in boxes to unpack later*." She is an actress, and it has been challenging not to be able to work. She wasn't looking for a career change but was forced to make one due to her accident; she has recently started doing voiceovers.

Jessica says that the accident has slowed her down and given her the time to consider anew what has meaning in her life. Her new mantra is "*enough*." Jessica has shifted her priorities to her own recovery, family, friends, and a new career. "It's no longer about a better vacation or a bigger house," she explains. Just after her accident she started a mindful awareness meditation practice and says it has been immensely helpful in adjusting to the changes in her life. While slowing down has been challenging for her, and it's still hard for her to watch her friends having kids, moving ahead in their careers, and traveling—all things she cannot do right now—she nonetheless notices a sense of calm and gratitude that she attributes to her daily practice. Hopefully, Jessica's story will inspire you, as it did me, to use Pacing to remind us to take time to consider whether our lives reflect what continues to have meaning for us, as we discussed in Part 2 on Purpose. Jessica also provides a beautiful example of how our well-being is not dependent upon our physical wellness. Well-being is a choice, like our happiness, which we are in charge of, no matter our health or other challenges in life.

The key is to be aware of the ebb and flow of life through Presence, keeping in mind that we can often set the pace that works best for us at any given time. The few minutes that I take each morning to meditate allow me to feel more in charge of my pace. It seems that those few moments come back to me many times over as I feel more calm throughout the day.

Transitions: The Spaces in Between

Irish poet John O'Donohue talked a great deal about transitions. He urged, for example, that we pay special attention to the first few hours in a new city or neighborhood, as we will observe things only at that time that we will soon take for granted or be unable to detect, even after just two or three days in a new place. *Treasuring the transitions between events provides the necessary space for reframing and rejuvenating.* Thoreau said, "Part of us awakes which slumbers all the rest of the day and night."

If you're like me, you sometimes tend to rush around, always squeezing in one more thing—which inevitably takes more time than expected. A wonderful Japanese word, *yuutori*, refers to the spaciousness we can enjoy when we arrive early for an appointment or meeting, with sufficient time to look around and not be in a rush. *Yuutori* is also the pause we often take after we read a poem, when we can hold the poem just as the poem holds us. My Japanese friend Keiko explains it this way: "It's very important for peace and enjoying life. You can't be busy minded always. It's a necessity, not a luxury. It's not wasting time." When we allow the extra time, we often don't think that we'll actually *need* it, but it's useful for the space and peace of mind it provides—and of course it comes in handy on occasions when we do actually need it.

On my recent visit to Japan, I enjoyed a relaxing day before my meetings. The unscheduled time to settle in was incredibly restorative; however, I must admit that I wouldn't ordinarily leave such space in my schedule. I would schedule every block of time, making the most of every moment, because after all, I'm in Japan. Having taken that transition time, however, made a difference for my entire trip. Similarly, even something as simple as a two- or three-minute walk before entering your apartment after a long day at work can reframe your state of mind and rejuvenate you. Or, a quick cup of your favorite beverage on your way to pick up your dad for his doctor's appointment can offer a welcome refresher.

Pacing Means Giving Yourself Permission to . . .

Pacing is also about giving ourselves permission. "Permission to do what?" you may be asking. Let's start with the following:

Permission to rest.

Permission to do less.

Permission to just be.

Permission to say no.

Permission to not fix it.

Permission to delegate.

Permission to set limits.

Permission to not excel.

Permission to do nothing.

Permission to see friends.

Permission to be yourself.

Permission to ask for help.

Permission to be guilt-free.

Permission to make a mistake.

Permission to take good care of ourselves.

Permission to not be Mom in all situations.

Permission to take the selfish out of self-care.

Permission to not feel responsible for everything.

What did you feel as you read this list? Is there something that you would like to give yourself permission to do? My mother-in-law, Sue, with a very satisfied look on her face recently announced to me the following: "Now at ninety, for the first time, I'm giving myself permission to do whatever I want, including nothing. That's a big deal. Next month when I resign after thirty years as a docent at the museum, I'm going to start saying no more often." How does that sound to you? It sounds great to me, and if you're like me, you'd also prefer not to wait until age ninety . . . so let's start now to give ourselves permission to live in ways that reflect what matters most to us.

Busy is not only often our default pace, but as I mentioned earlier, it's often associated with success. Our weekdays can be so overscheduled that weekends offer a welcome respite, a much-needed change of pace to have (almost) nothing scheduled. On such weekends we can enjoy the luxury of time to be open to whatever comes up—and perhaps most important of all, we can give ourselves permission to rest. A few months ago, a three-day weekend loomed large in my imagination. All during my hectic workweek, I made lists and looked to those three days to completely catch up. When the end of day three of the long weekend came around, I realized that I hadn't done even one thing on my list.

What happened to the vanishing time? I think I played hooky on myself. In fact, I hadn't even looked at my list. I harvested the oranges from our backyard tree, enjoyed the afternoon's blue sky, and other than that I cannot tell you what I did. Looking back, I think that my real priority for that weekend was a personal recharge, and although my body was on board with that, my mind was the last to know. Next time, I hope I can give myself permission in advance to take the weekend off.

Permission to recharge is also important when we're traveling. When our children were young, Dan and I took them to London and looked forward to showing them Big Ben and other highlights, but one day neither of them wanted to leave the hotel. I thought that was such a waste of our time in London. However, Dan and the children viewed it differently, so that day they stayed in the hotel and made paper dolls while I went out to explore London. It wasn't what we had planned, but a reframe helped us adjust to how the day would look. In the end, the day off restored the children's energy level, and the next day we all happily left the hotel to visit Big Ben.

Rest restores our energy, helps us focus on what matters while avoiding things that don't matter. Alex Soojung-Kim Pang, founder of the Restful Company, explains, *"When we treat rest as work's equal and partner . . . we elevate rest into something that can help calm our days, organize our lives, give us more time, and help us achieve more while working less"* (italics mine). Pang recognizes that rest is often mistaken for idleness but explains that they are different as follows: "Resting as in watching clouds float across the sky or listening to a waterfall is not a waste of time. Idleness, as in indolence, laziness, or sluggishness, is a source of misery, whereas rest is a source of happiness."

Here's a story about rest from the German writer Heinrich Böll, published in 1953, about a visitor to a small fishing village along the western coast of Europe. The visitor spots a seemingly "lazy" local fisherman resting in his boat, and he asks impatiently why the fisherman doesn't spend more time fishing, so that he could catch more,

Pacing means gifting yourself permission to . . .

build his business, and ultimately enjoy some vacation time. The fisherman points out that with no pressure to constantly build his business, he is free and has already what so many seek: time for friendship, rest, and community.

Saying No

For many of us, it isn't easy to say no. Do any of these sound familiar to you? "I don't want to disappoint anyone," "I can't let them down," "I won't be asked again," "They won't like me," or "I'll jeopardize my reputation." Why are we so reluctant to say no? We all have our reasons for why we hesitate when what we really want to do is say no. Sociologist Christine Carter explains that we aren't taught to say no because it's "a rebuff, a rebuttal, a minor act of verbal violence. 'No' is for drugs and strangers with candy." Mary Pipher said that the first time she said no, she thought "lightning would strike!" She recalled how she was raised with a "your wish is my command" mentality; in other words, being available to others and not affirming her own needs.

Saying no becomes more difficult with FOMO, or fear of missing out. You'll remember that Sue, my mother-in-law, finally at age ninety was going to start saying no more often. A few months later when I asked Sue how it was going, she had this modification: "When you are in your eighties and nineties, you're so happy to be asked to do things. It gets more complicated to say no because you want to stay engaged, busy, and connected. You'd never want to be convicted of being old or suffering from aging!"

Furthermore, from an early age, we have been socialized to say yes, in order to keep the peace and put others' needs first. Coupled with this is our perceived ability to do nearly everything without stopping to consider how realistic it is to do everything; as a result, we equate "I can do it" with "*I should do it*." One of the real downsides of saying yes too often is that when things we really want to do come our way, we can't do them because we have no time. Saying yes to one thing may necessitate saying no to another, while saying no to one thing means that we can say yes to something else.

Isabella, a forty-five-year-old mom of two teenagers, has worked as a nanny for the past twenty years. Having completed only a sixth-grade education in her native Belize, she now aspires to earn her GED since her sons are through college. To pursue this, however, she had to resign from her longtime position as volunteer soccer commissioner, which she found difficult to do. When she announced her resignation, she was met with resistance from the other parents, such as: "But you are so good at it!" and "No one can take your place!" Fortunately, Isabella had already made a firm decision and was not swayed; her priority had shifted to her own education and she had the strength to say no.

Another challenge in saying no is that we are often committing to something seemingly so far in the future that we're sure we can safely say yes. Somehow the future promises to hold more time for all of us, in spite of the fact that few of us have ever found that to be true. So we agree to take the lead on several projects at work over the next few months, chair the school's fund-raiser in the fall, and organize our family's annual summer reunion. How do we say no more often and sooner? And without second-guessing ourselves or feeling guilty? One way is to have a look at your current day or week and consider how it would feel to have the deadline upon you today, tomorrow, or even next week. You will likely feel relieved that this particular event is not approaching next week or even within the next two weeks. Chances are that the availability in your calendar a few weeks or months from now will not be significantly different than it is right now; different commitments, perhaps, but the same level of intensity likely lies ahead. I encourage you to ask yourself, "How would I manage this today?" the next time you are asked to take on something beyond your usual commitments.

Another important part of learning to say no is preparing to say no. Don't be caught off guard! Sociologist Christine Carter, author of *The Sweet Spot* and *Raising Happiness*, urges us to have a line ready for conveying a gentle no. Maybe something along the lines of "Thank you so much for asking, but that isn't going to work out for me right now." She even suggests that we follow author Peter Bregman's advice and simply pick our top five priorities and then spend 95 percent of our time doing *only* those activities. Carter tried this out for herself, and at first it seemed impossible to do, but she now understands that the key to sticking to our top five priorities is to align them with our values and greater Purpose, and then it's entirely possible to say no to everything else.

Our engaged lives mean that there will always be times when we find ourselves feeling overwhelmed, even with saying no more frequently. However, the more we can be aware of our reasons for saying yes and our Purpose, the more likely we can have the time we need for what matters most to us.

Several weeks ago, I had invited two friends to my house for dinner to celebrate a birthday that ends in a zero for one of them. Two days before the party, I thought I should cancel or at least postpone it since I had so much to do. Then I remembered why the date was set up in the first place—because I value the friendships, which span over twenty years. The date had been on my calendar for weeks, and the three of us live in different cities and rarely meet. I asked myself, "Isn't maintaining my friendships one of the most important things I can do for my well-being?" Once I reframed the plan this way, reconnecting with my Purpose, I felt calmer and grateful for the time I would have with my friends.

FEELING OVERWHELMED?

Breathe.

Don't engage.

Get some fresh air.

Step away from the drama.

Do only one thing at a time.

Remember: Not my monkeys, not my circus.

The Myth of Multitasking

Many of us believe we are pretty good, if not masters, at multitasking, and perhaps some of us consider it our most important survival tool. But it turns out that we have the capacity to do only one task that requires our attention at a time. Here's how the brain works when it comes to multitasking: We have what's called intermittent partial attention. If you place three things into your working memory, your brain will process them one by one. Try as we might, we can't override this. What does this mean? It means that the brain doesn't multitask, but rather switches rapidly from one thing to the next. Following each switch, when our attention returns to the original task, the strength of our attention has been appreciably diminished and it can take several minutes to ramp up again to full concentration.

Neuroscientist Amishi Jha calls our working memory the mind's whiteboard, the place where the information our attention selects gets parked for our use. Scientists used to think that our working memory could hold seven things, plus or minus one or two more, but now the number has been adjusted to just three to five things. Working memory works quickly—things are only present for about thirty seconds. No wonder things vanish from our radar even with the best of our intentions; we are up against disappearing ink! Our whiteboard gets rewritten as soon as we hit the maximum of three to five items, which—if your life is like mine—happens within seconds.

When we multitask, we are inefficient because when we do more than one task at a time, we aren't able to do either task well. Multitasking also makes us unable to remember if we did a certain thing. Have you ever thought you sent an email, but it turned out that you didn't? I know this is bad news for those of you who rely heavily on multitasking to get through your hectic days. I'm not saying that we can't do a couple of things simultaneously that don't require too much concentration, but when it comes to demanding tasks that require our full attention, multitasking doesn't serve us well.

Computer scientist Cal Newport distinguishes what he calls "deep work," focusing without distraction on a cognitively demanding task, from "shallow work," which includes sending emails and answering calls. Newport says, *"Even when people think that they're single-tasking, what they're still doing is every five or ten minutes a 'just-check' . . . but even those very brief checks that switch your context even briefly can have this massive negative impact on your cognitive performance"* (italics mine). Deep work happens only when we take the time to sit down with one single problem and work without distraction. If we start multitasking, we will need time to start again. If we are distracted, we will get nothing meaningful done.

Multitasking v. Single-tasking

Newport recommends scheduling time to do simple tasks, like answering emails into blocks, just as we would with meetings, to ensure that we dedicate ourselves to only one task at a time.

Titrating the Tech

We are constantly barraged by news, push notifications, and enticing ads all skillfully competing for two of our limited resources: our time and our attention. Our human ability to create is faster than our ability to adapt. Can we ever adapt to 24/7 demands? Do we want to adapt to 24/7 demands? How can we keep up with our virtual and our real lives? We don't easily set our devices aside, whether it's our smartphone, iPad, or laptop; they serve as a magnetic force that pulls us out of the present moment and consumes our precious time. Unfortunately, our devices don't come with rules for usage, but rules do emerge informally from the various settings we find ourselves in daily. Studies show, for example, that as soon as one person checks her device, others feel empowered to do the same.

Gopi Kallayil at Google is a leading voice encouraging mindfulness in the workplace and likens our cell phones to our 207th body part.

Workplace expectations regarding connectivity after hours or during vacations vary widely from company to company, and even among departments within a given company. One interviewee, Jackie, shared with me that her supervisor said he didn't expect her to check her email on weekends, while warning her that she "shouldn't miss an email from Walter," her supervisor's boss who is infamous for sending emails at all hours and expecting a response within minutes. One study on such workplaces found that establishing healthier boundaries between work and outside life would benefit companies by way of employees' mental health: "If employees felt free to draw some lines between their professional and personal lives, organizations would benefit from greater engagement, more open relationships, and more paths to success."

Some countries are not leaving it to businesses to set their own expectations when it comes to after-hours email. France, for example, recently passed legislation that employers cannot expect employees to check their email outside normal business hours. Our pervasive connectivity has also made its way into our schools, with teachers and administrators growing increasingly concerned about cell phone use. Many U.S. schools have issued policies to regulate cell phone use, or have even banned them during school hours, while others issue their students see-through "security pouches" each morning to keep their devices inoperable but by their side. Transparent pouches are a compromise, due to an increase in anxiety when children are separated from their devices.

Restrictions on device use in some countries are even more stringent. France recently passed a law banning students ages three to fifteen from using smartphones anywhere on school grounds, with few exceptions. The education ministry has also recommended that schools install lockers where students can deposit their phones for the day. These regulations are a response to the consistent rise of usage among children; in 2017, nearly 80 percent of people in the United States age twelve to seventeen had a smartphone, and in France, 86 percent of people in the same age range had a smartphone.

Inner-net is a term coined by Kallayil to describe our inner technologies (our mind and body). Kallayil says, "The most important technology every single person gets to use every single day is inside of us—starting with our brain, starting with our breathing." He urges us to unplug from our devices in order to plug into ourselves, allowing space for practicing Presence and reconnecting with our bodies and minds. In this way, we can better manage the deluge of distractions. In our family, the Internet is affectionately referred to as the "infinet"—since there is always something more to explore and we are never done. The infinet, as it were, also gives us a sense of insufficiency and urgency to keep up—which is futile and can give rise, if we don't consider Pacing, to a sense of helplessness and inadequacy.

Unplug from Devices and Plug into Now

Regulating how and when we use our devices is one practical step we can take in Pacing ourselves when it comes to technology, not only so that we can protect our limited natural resources of attention and time, but also for our well-being. As I mentioned, 70 percent of us sleep with our phones; we can improve our well-being by keeping our phones off of our nightstands. Here's how it works: The biggest spike of cortisol for the day occurs in the first fifteen minutes of waking up, and that spike determines how much our cortisol overshoots for the remainder of the day. If we wake up and grab our phones, only to be bombarded with news and demands, our cortisol level will be high. One friend told me that within five minutes of waking each morning, she gets online and starts trading. Imagine her cortisol levels! Alternatively, if we wake up more peacefully, we'll have higher levels of telomerase, and in turn increase our health and longevity. Arianna Huffington makes space for joy each morning by separating herself from her devices. As she explains it, in this way, when we wake up, we'll have some time to breathe and establish our intention for the day.

Is It a Pebble, a Rock, or a Boulder?

I have a thirteen-year-old friend and neighbor named Lily. A few years ago, I had the fun of attending her fourth-grade class presentation on problem solving where the teacher provided this prompt to the students: "Do we have a pebble, a rock, or a boulder on our hands?" The teacher was illustrating for the class the importance of assessing the nature and size of a problem before taking action. Upon hearing this, I thought about how relevant this is to Pacing. To my peril, I sometimes give wildly different demands and problems the same level of attention, which often means going full speed ahead on just about everything. Maybe this is your inclination, too. After all, many of us like getting things done so we can cross them off our lists—better now than later.

Recently, I have been working on trying to slow down and determine, case by case, how much is required of me. I also ask myself, "When can I realistically devote the attention needed to the task, considering the brainpower and emotional energy needed?" Conjuring up the images of a pebble, a rock, and a boulder has been very helpful. Other questions include looking at what a given project will require—minimal, medium, or substantial attention and energy? How urgent is it? I've also found that more and more things can wait, and when I do get to them, they are often less daunting than they previously were (remember our friend "selective neglect"). Some of them even disappear! The following table gives a road map for Pacing. (Yes, I realize that most of the answers are additional questions!)

PACING ROAD MAP: YOU'RE IN THE DRIVER'S SEAT	
Questions	Answers
Is it a pebble, a rock, or a boulder?	What resources will this responsibility require?
What's the deadline?	How does this deadline fit into your schedule?
What's the time required?	Reserve a realistic amount of time for a good enough, not perfect, response.
Are you holding anyone up?	What's the impact on others if you don't act promptly?
Remember: Take time to pace yourself.	

Cumulative Leveling

I coined the term *cumulative leveling* as an antidote to the elusive concept of balance. Cumulative leveling expands our time frame by weeks, months, or even years. We've talked about how our lives are messy, and balancing suggests managing just two things, which is rarely the case for any of us. On top of that, if we tend to look at a single day to determine whether we've been able to live consistently with our Purpose or Purposes in life, we will likely be disappointed often. While illusory day-to-day, we can appreciate and realize that we are honoring various of our life Purposes when we expand the time frame. With the metric of a month rather than a week, for example, we can more readily appreciate that we are moving forward in furtherance of our purposes, thanks to the longer time frame.

As Stacy, the former newspaper editor in Chicago whom I introduced earlier, describes it: "One day you're killing it at work but don't get home to dinner with your kids and feel like a failure as a mom, and the next day you have a slow day at work, arrive home in time to take the kids to the playground, and feel like a great mom." The ability to step back and view our days with a wider lens can make all the difference in how we feel about our management of our various roles.

Similarly, Shannon, the consultant and mom of two whom I mentioned earlier, has this to say about balance: "I don't use the word *balance* anymore. It's about choices. It's so important to right-size your path. When I'm out of town for a week on business, it's nonstop and I'm working twelve- to fourteen-hour days. I'm not thinking about balance. I'm thinking: *I've made a choice to take this business trip. Next week I'll have more time with my kids.* My metric isn't day-by-day; it's week-by-week, and sometimes month-by-month. As long as I can look at each day and know why it is as it is, I am OK."

Now is a good time to see for yourself how this works. Review your day and consider whether you were able to incorporate a few of the undertakings that are in furtherance of your life's Purposes. Now expand your lens to one week or one month, and see if you can appreciate the difference.

Big Birthdays and the Ones in Between

As I mentioned earlier, our chronological ages don't define us. One woman whom I interviewed, a recently divorced thirty-one-year-old, told me that she felt "young at age thirty-one, but while still unhappily married at age twenty-eight," she felt old. Another woman said, "At twenty-nine I felt so young, and at thirty I feel all of this pressure." Several women in their forties whom I interviewed exclaimed, "I'm so happy to be done with my twenties and thirties!" One thirty-nine-year-old said, "I like being on the verge of forty, but it doesn't feel like thirty! I'm ready for forty. Good-bye to all of that uncertainty about what my career will look like, kids or not, spouse or not, where to live. . . . I'm relieved that all of those vexing decisions are behind me now." I interviewed fifty-year-olds who felt "finished" in their careers, sixty-year-olds just starting jobs in new fields, seventy-year-olds who thought things would be "slowing down by now but they haven't," and eighty-year-olds who feel too young to be taking classes for seniors at their local college.

Birthdays are a time when we may feel a sense of transience and impermanence. We may feel especially vulnerable when we are approaching a big birthday, particularly one ending in zero that may be anticipated for months or even years and accompanied by plenty of expectations. When it comes to Pacing, birthdays can provide an opportunity to reflect on our lives and ask questions such as "What life chapter am I in right now?" and "When I take a long view of my life, are there things that I'm trying to fit in right now that can wait?" And of course questions about Pacing necessarily include questions about Purpose as well, such as "What has meaning for me right now?" and "Am I living consistent with my Purpose?"

That was certainly true for Stephanie, who was about to turn forty and had finally found work she loves in Aurora, Colorado, as a physical therapist. She and her husband, a salesman for a local oil and gas company, together with their three teenage children, bought their first house. However, over the past year, Stephanie began to realize that she wasn't comfortable with the financial pressures that came along with owning her dream home. Finally, Stephanie couldn't take it anymore so she and her husband went apartment hunting. Within one month of Stephanie's fortieth birthday, they sold their house and moved. When I asked Stephanie how she made sense of her move, she said that as she looked ahead to turning forty, she felt it was "about time" that she and her husband owned their own home and felt that was her "next adult move." Some of us may have at one time or another attached a milestone marker to a given life stage or chronological age as Stephanie did. The key is to continue to use the power of Presence and ask ourselves the important questions about Purpose, Pivoting, and Pacing—and it need not be just at the time of a birthday!

Here's some good news for those of you approaching your sixties. We've discussed the negativity bias we all share, where positive things have less impact on our behavior than things that are equally emotional but negative. However, *as we approach our sixties and beyond, studies show that our brains will become happier.* Research has found that older age is associated with higher levels of overall satisfaction, happiness, and well-being, and lower levels of anxiety, depression, and stress. The older we are, the better our mental health.

According to psychologist Laura Carstensen, *the sweet spot for our happiness is in our late sixties to early seventies*. As we move through our decades, Carstensen explains that we experience what she calls "a positivity effect." We tend to stop and appreciate things more, primarily our relationships and the present moment. Compared with young people, middle-aged and older people tend to look at the glass as half-full; they seem to bounce back from adversity more quickly and get better at living in the present by focusing on what matters most right now. Carstensen says, "When people face endings they tend to shift from goals about exploration and expanding horizons to ones about savoring relationships and focusing on meaningful activities. When you focus on emotionally meaningful goals, life gets better, you feel better, and the negative emotions become less frequent and more fleeting when they occur."

Here's more good news: *There is almost no hard evidence for the so-called midlife crisis*. Research across life spans shows midlife and beyond to be more about *renewal* than *crisis*. It's a time of pausing or shifting gears (as we discussed in Part 3 on Pivoting), but certainly not a time of prolonged or permanent stall, much less crisis. Midlife is an exhilarating time; with experience behind us and promise in the future, we are in a unique place in our lives. As Barbara Hagerty says, "I have come to believe that the forties, fifties, and sixties are the least understood and, in some ways, the most critical phase of life. *Midlife is not flyover territory*" (italics mine). Hagerty also points out that, historically, any significant event such as an accident, sickness, divorce, a parent dying, or a child leaving for college were all labeled a "midlife crisis" if they happened during midlife, but in fact, these events can happen at any time in life, and research shows that the biggest upheavals in career and family occur *before age forty*.

Not only is the midlife crisis nonexistent, but we can develop more resilience as we age—which is especially helpful since many of life's biggest challenges seem to cluster in midlife. As Hagerty explains, "[We] are more likely to lose a parent or spouse after forty, more likely to be diagnosed with cancer after forty-five, and much more likely to be replaced by a younger, cheaper, more tech-savvy employee after fifty." We've talked a lot about bringing forward our most resilient selves and some research suggests that as we age, there is a natural increase in resilience. As neuroscientist Richard Davidson says, "As people get older, they have more experience under their belts. They learn through their experience to better regulate their emotions. They also learn the challenges that they confront are not the end of the world, and that life will go on."

I imagine we can all agree that our health is more important than chronological age. We often continue to feel young until we face a major health crisis or the loss of a loved one. Developmental psychologist Bernice Neugarten makes a distinction between young-old age and what she calls old-old age, which is when our health fundamentally changes the way we live. Mary Pipher, in *Women Rowing North*, describes aging this way: "With each new stage of life, we outgrow the strategies that worked for us at an earlier stage. . . . To be happy at this junction, we cannot just settle for being a diminished version of our younger selves . . . we add new aspects and expand on many others. We learn to balance the loss of certain roles with the crafting of fresh and more serviceable ones. *Hopefully, we become more gentle and kind to ourselves*" (italics mine). As this is the next to last section of the book, it's fitting to end with Mary Pipher's reference to our being more gentle and kind to ourselves, just where we began our conversation.

Pacing in Brief

The antidote to "doing it all, all at once" for any age and stage of our lives is Pacing. With ever-increasing health spans, we can now enjoy more time than ever for pursuing multiple personal and professional interests. The key is to focus our limited resources of time and attention on what matters most to us right now—knowing that with Pacing there will be more time in a later chapter of life to shift our focus to other Purposes. This long view of our lives can liberate us from feeling the urgency and being overwhelmed so many of us experience when we put pressure on ourselves to try to fit too many endeavors in one phase of our lives. Pacing also helps us to set a pace that makes sense for us, through practical ways, which include saying no more often, assessing how much time and energy a given challenge will require of us, and imposing rules on our devices. Remember, you set the pace.

6 FEATURES OF PACING

Set your own pace.

Recognize what life stage you are in.

Embrace the bumps along the way.

Realize you really can't do everything.

Take the long view of your life.

Focus your limited resource of attention on what matters most.

Self-Compassion Practices

As we arrive at the last two meditations, let's circle back to where we started our journey together. We've explored how we are often our own inner critic rather than ally, placing unrealistic expectations on ourselves and feeling that we are somehow falling short no matter our bounty. I can leave you with no more powerful gifts than two self-compassion practices so that you have a place to turn when you are not treating yourself the way you would treat your best friend. The first practice is called "Time for Kindness" and is inspired by Neff's three components of self-compassion that I mentioned earlier (self-kindness, common humanity, and mindfulness).

TIME FOR KINDNESS

- Sit comfortably, or lie down.

- Gently close your eyes completely or partially.

- This is your time.

- Treasure it and protect it.

- Open your awareness to the sensations of your body.

- Take a deep breath.

- There's no need to rush right now.

- Bring to mind a challenge, a struggle, or situation that is bothering you.

- Starting with mindful awareness, just notice how your body feels when you think of this challenge.

- Let yourself be with the sensations you feel in your body.

- Just be with what already is.

- No need to ignore or push away what you are feeling.

- Just make space for whatever you are feeling.

- Say a few words to yourself, such as "This is incredibly difficult," or "I'm having such a rough time right now."

- Let these sensations of acceptance and words of comfort sink in.

- Be fully present in this moment.

- Now recognize that each of us faces challenges such as this, at one time or another.

- This is what it means to be a part of our human family.

- Say a few words which remind you that you are not alone, such as "Others feel the same way I do," or "This is just a natural part of life."

- Let these words sink in.

- Bringing the challenge to mind again, are you blaming yourself and feeling that what's happening is somehow your fault?

- Remember, no need to evaluate or judge.

- You can be supportive and kind to yourself, just as you would for a friend in a similar situation, and say a few words, such as, "I care about you," or "I'm right here for you."

- Feel free to add physical touch that is comforting to you. For example, place your hand over your heart or give yourself a gentle hug.

- As we get ready to close, remember that you can return to this practice at any time.

- Commit to turning to yourself with kindness as often as needed throughout the day.

- Whenever you're ready, slowly open your eyes.

~~~~~~~~~~~~~~~~~~~~~~~~~~~~~~~~~~~

The RAIN of Self-Compassion Practice

The second self-compassion practice that you may find useful when you feel overwhelmed or not good enough is called "RAIN," a simple practice available 24/7 and very easy to remember! Meditation teacher Michele McDonald first coined the acronym RAIN more than twenty years ago and it's still circulating in meditation communities in various forms. The one I'm including here is a version mindfulness teacher Tara Brach calls the RAIN of Self-Compassion. In her decades of work with tens of thousands of clients and meditation students, Brach has observed that a sense of personal deficiency is epidemic and says that when we feel unworthy we are "in a trance that causes tremendous suffering."

The "R" of RAIN stands for Recognize what's going on. Common signs of the trance Brach is referring to include a critical inner voice, anxiety, feelings of shame or fear, or the weight of depression in the body. The first step out of the trance of unworthiness is simply to recognize that we are stuck.

The "A" of RAIN stands for Allow the experience to be here, just as it is. We don't need to fix anything or avoid our thoughts and feelings. When caught in self-judgment, letting it be doesn't mean we agree with our belief that we're unworthy, it's simply acknowledging the arising of our judgment, as well as the pain we feel.

The "I" of RAIN stands for Investigate gently and with care. After we have recognized and allowed whatever is arising, we can deepen our attention by turning inward and asking, "How am I experiencing this in my body right now?" Investigating is not about figuring out the cause of our suffering; rather, it is meant to be somatic. Brach encourages investigating with kindness and without judgment so that we can create a sufficient sense of safety in order to truly connect with our fears, hurts, and shame.

This brings us to the "N" of RAIN, which in some versions of RAIN stands for Non-identification; that is, our sense of who we are is not fused with our thoughts, feelings, and sensations. However, in Brach's RAIN of Self-Compassion, "N" stands for Nurture with Self-Compassion since she has found that the RAIN Practice is more transformative for her students when a full step is devoted to self-compassion. While self-compassion naturally arises when we recognize that we are suffering, Brach explains that "[i]t comes into fullness when we intentionally nurture our inner life with self-care."

Try to sense your most vulnerable part, where you feel the worst, and what's needed right now. A gesture of care, which may include saying a phrase such as, "I'm listening," or "It's not your fault," placing your hand on your heart, or envisioning being bathed in warm sunlight, can be very comforting and healing. If it's too hard to offer such kindness and love to yourself, bring to mind a loving being in your life, perhaps a friend or pet, and imagine that being's love surrounding you. Just the intention to offer care to ourselves starts to decrease our tendency to diminish ourselves.

After completing the four active steps of RAIN, take time to simply notice your own Presence, resting in open awareness, no longer imprisoned by the trance of unworthiness, and unhelpful beliefs and attitudes.

THE RAIN OF SELF-COMPASSION PRACTICE

Recognize what's going on

Allow the experience to be here, just as it is

Investigate gently and with care

Nurture with self-compassion

After the **RAIN**, rest in open awareness, noticing your own presence

EVERYDAY PRINCIPLES OF PRESENCE

It's OK to say no.

Change is constant.

Now is a good time.

Trust what you feel.

Self-care is not selfish.

Comparison is the thief of all joy.

Good friendships are worth the energy.

A small change can make a big difference.

Twenty Suggestions
for Living with Presence

Thank you for having trusted me with your time in the journey of reading this book. I hope that something in these pages has made you feel "six inches taller," as one of my students put it after attending one of my weekend workshops. I also hope that in some small ways you are already experiencing more Presence, perhaps by noticing a buffer so that you may more often respond, not react, or feeling in closer touch with your life's Purpose, or seeing more options in your life by Pivoting—before absolutely necessary—or using Pacing as a gentle reminder that at this particular time in your life, you are exactly where you should be. Yes, that one is worth repeating to yourself: "I am exactly where I should be."

As you move forward, here are twenty suggestions for enjoying more Presence that can illuminate and inform not only your life's Purpose, but also your decisions when it comes to Pivoting and Pacing.

I trust they will provide touchstones for you along your journey.

On the Power of Presence

- If you are like the rest of us, which is to say human, you may often experience a busy mind that is prone to wandering. The key is to bring your attention back to the present moment, for as many moments as possible throughout the day.

* One or two breaths at a time, one or two moments whenever and wherever you can, all serve to bring you into the present. No one moment is more important than another.

* We can't change others, nor can we change world events, but we can change our relationship to both. And that's where the transformative power of Presence lies.

* Emotions come and go unless we try to push them away or cling to them.

* Stress is an inherent part of our engaged lives of meaning. Reframing how we *think* of stress profoundly changes whether stress impacts us in a positive or negative way.

* Our thoughts may or may not be true.

* Living with more Presence means more choices.

* Presence is not a panacea, but it can lay the foundation for small, powerful, and lasting changes in our lives.

On Presence and Purpose

* Finding and having Purpose in life starts with Presence. Our Purpose provides direction and meaning in our lives. Purpose arises out of what's personally significant to us and has an impact beyond ourselves.

* Purpose is not a luxury, only for the privileged. It's free, available 24/7, and a necessity for well-being for each of us.

* Our lives are complex and we all have difficult, discouraging days, but Purpose can keep us going during our most challenging times.

- Purpose can be uncoupled from passion. Many of us may be unable to identify a passion, but nonetheless we can live purposeful lives.

On Presence and Pivoting

- Pivoting starts with Presence. Only by knowing what we're experiencing and what's most important to us can we determine whether or not we need to make a change in our life.
- Our human nature is to resist change and avoid uncertainty; however, Pivoting *before* absolutely necessary usually means having more options.
- All of our resources, including experiences and relationships, support us before, during, and after Pivoting.
- There are no perfect decisions, only empowered ones.

On Presence and Pacing

- Pacing starts with Presence. Only with an open and clear mind can we discern our priorities in order to pace ourselves.
- While most of us think that we are great at multitasking, our brain actually cannot simultaneously process multiple tasks, but rather switches rapidly from one task to the next. When returning our attention to a previous task, it can take several minutes to ramp up again to full concentration.
- Allowing transition time between events is not wasted time, but rather necessary for rejuvenation.
- Digital media bombards us and Pacing invites us to regulate our intake. Remember, we don't need to respond to everything.

FURTHER RESOURCES

Let's Talk More

We're just getting started. I look forward to continuing our conversation at carolinewelch.com and facebook.com/carolinewelch author. Also, I invite you to start or join a Presence Group at www.carolinewelch.com/presence-groups (yes, in person!). No matter your age or location, now is a good time to come together to explore, support, and share ideas on how Presence and the 3 Ps can make a difference in your life.

Recommended Reading

For the latest Recommended Reading list, please visit: www.carolinewelch.com/recommended-reading.

A Sampling of Mindfulness Resources

1440 Multiversity: https://1440.org/

Tara Brach's Resources: https://www.tarabrach.com/

Dr. Judson Brewer's lab: https://www.brown.edu/academics /public-health/research/mindfulness/

Center for Compassion and Altruism Research and Education, Stanford University: http://ccare.stanford.edu

Center for Healthy Minds, University of Wisconsin–Madison: https://centerhealthyminds.org

Dr. Elissa Epel's lab: http://www.amecenter.ucsf.edu

The Garrison Institute: https://www.garrisoninstitute.org/

Greater Good Science Center, University of California at Berkeley: https://greatergood.berkeley.edu

InsightLA Meditation: https://insightla.org/

Insight Meditation Society: https://www.dharma.org/

Dr. Amishi Jha's lab: http://www.amishi.com/lab/

Jon Kabat-Zinn's Guided Meditations: https://www.mindfulnesscds.com/

Jack Kornfield's Resources: https://jackkornfield.com/

MARC at UCLA: https://www.uclahealth.org/marc/

Mind & Life Institute: https://mindandlife.org

Mindfulness-Based Cognitive Therapy: http://mbct.com

Mindsight Institute Online Courses and Workshops:
https://www.mindsightinstitute.com

National Center for Complementary and Integrative Health:
https://nccih.nih.gov

Omega Institute: https://www.eomega.org/

Dr. Dan Siegel's Resources: http://www.drdansiegel.com/press/

Sounds True: https://www.soundstrue.com/store/

Spirit Rock: https://www.spiritrock.org/

UCLA Mindful Awareness Research Center: http://marc.ucla.edu

ACKNOWLEDGMENTS

My work at the Mindsight Institute over the past dozen years, together with my mindfulness practice that began more than forty years ago when I was living in Japan, provided the impetus for this book.

I am grateful to my editor, Sara Carder of TarcherPerigee at Penguin Random House, who for years had faith in my writing and waited patiently until finally I was ready to write my first book. I feel so fortunate to have benefited from her vision, encouragement, and more than twenty years of publishing experience. Editorial assistant extraordinaire Rachel Ayotte was wonderful to work with, answered every question, and kept me right on schedule. Copy editor Amy Schneider was highly skillful at improving upon every detail. Deep thanks to publisher Megan Newman; production manager Anne Chan; production editor Claire Winecoff; interior designer Elke Sigal; cover designer Jess Morphew and her team; and the publicity and marketing team of Casey Maloney, Farin Schlussel, Sara Johnson, and Carla Iannone.

My literary agent, Joelle Delbourgo, resonated with this project from the start and has been invaluable in guiding my writing and editing. Joelle provided a calm, good-humored, optimistic Presence, which I've treasured throughout the process.

I'm also grateful to Elissa Epel, who insisted that I jump-start the book by going on a writing retreat, which turned out to be the only way that I could not only begin writing but also sustain it through to the finish. Many thanks to my cousin Katherine Eskovitz for fine-tuning the topic with me one sunny morning at our neighborhood coffee shop. I'm also thankful to Diane Ackerman, who read part of what some writers accurately call the "silly first draft" and had nothing but encouraging words.

Deep thanks also to Susan Kaiser Greenland, who told me that not writing is also writing. This didn't make much sense when she first said it, but I came to appreciate the importance of letting ideas simmer. I am also grateful to Kate Capshaw for sharing the wisdom of how to move on from a book or any work of art. Without that perspective, I might still be writing.

The scientific sources are too numerous to list here, but I am deeply grateful for all of the valuable work that is being done each day to expand our knowledge. Graduate students Talya Vogel, researcher on meaning at PGSP-Stanford Psy.D. Consortium, and Ellie Weisbaum, mindfulness researcher at the University of Toronto, reviewed drafts at critical stages and helped me hone my understanding of not only Presence and Purpose, but also the relationship between them.

I'm grateful for the mindfulness teachers, researchers, and poets who provide us with inspiration and insights, some of whose words permeate these pages. Special thanks to Tara Brach, Simone Humphrey, Kristin Neff, Sharon Salzberg, Zindel Segal, Dan Siegel, Signe Simon, John Teasdale, and Mark Williams, whose mindfulness practices are included here.

Special thanks to Julia Willinger for referring me to the perfect illustrator for this work, Carolyn Arcabascio. Carolyn's creativity has beautifully brought to life some of the book's abstract concepts, and working with her has been amazing. Laura Alvarez, Kristine Daily, and Madeleine Siegel shared their design talent and provided timely feedback as the illustrations were taking shape.

I admire and appreciate the candor, vulnerability, and collective wisdom of the more than one hundred women whom I interviewed about their experiences with Presence, Purpose, Pivoting, and Pacing. Although the majority preferred anonymity, some are named in the work, including Cate Furay, Trudy Goodman, Mimi Guarneri, Sky Jarrett, Amishi Jha, Sará King, Razeea Lemaignen, Rhonda Magee, Pamela McCauley, Peggy O'Kane, Sharon Salzberg, Shauna Shapiro, Ruchika Sikri, and Marie Tsuruda. While I couldn't include every one of the empowering stories I heard, the spirit of each of them has informed and inspired my work.

Writing a book is largely a solitary activity. These organizations were among those that provided opportunities for me to share and exchange ideas with scholars and students over the past five years, including The Art and Benefit of Mindfulness at the Brahm Center, Singapore; Center for Research in Neuropsychology and Cognitive Behavioral Intervention, University of Coimbra, Portugal; CIMBA Italy; Early Childhood Learning and Development Conference in Perth, Australia; the annual Mindful Leadership Summits in Washington, D.C.; the 1440 Multiversity in Scotts Valley, California; and the annual Psychotherapy Networker Conferences in Washington, D.C.

Support came in a variety of forms: from my circle of strong women whom I can always count on to the ad hoc title and book cover committees comprised of colleagues, former students, family, friends, artists, graphic designers, and my two book groups. Many thanks for taking the time on a moment's notice to email your feedback. Also sacred spaces for writing are essential. Deep thanks to Joanie and Scott Kriens for their vision in creating the 1440 Multiversity in the California redwoods, which provides an ideal environment for creative work. I am also deeply grateful to Cindy Winebaum for generously offering a writing sanctuary, just a quick drive from my office.

Jenn Bleyer, Katherine Eskovitz, Laura Hubber, and Madeleine Siegel brought their immense editorial talents to the manuscript. Their unvarnished, incisive, comprehensive comments, including line-by-line edits, profoundly shaped the work and helped me discover the book's final structure. My deepest thanks also go to several others who read drafts at various junctures and shared their discerning reflections, including Debra Crow, Jenny Lorant, Deena Margolin, Sue Siegel, Jennifer Taub, and Alta Tseng.

I'm also grateful for my team at the Mindsight Institute. Kayla Newcomer worked tirelessly as my research assistant and sounding board for two years. Phoebe Kiekhofer was a masterful editor at a critical phase in the manuscript's development; Kristi Morelli brought a clear mind and fresh eyes to the manuscript in its final editing phases; and Alexandra O'Brien meticulously managed the citations and multiple versions of the manuscript. Deep thanks also to Adriana Copeland, Jane Daily, Andrew Schulman, Ashish Soni, and Priscilla Vega for their enduring support.

My dreams for this book could not have come to fruition without the love, joy, and inspiration of my wonderful family during the many seasons of the writing process. My son, Alexander, provided a continual source of encouragement, which included weighing in on titles and cover designs. My daughter, Madeleine, offered an unwavering willingness to discuss ideas and review drafts. Her texts, such as "You got this, Mama," seemed to arrive just at the right times and kept me going. My life and work partner, Dan Siegel, source of up-to-the-minute neuroscience, had the patience to answer my endless questions as I worked out how to convey the science in an accurate, accessible way. It was usually a sign that we were in for a long discussion when in response to one of my questions, Dan would say something like, "Well, that's interesting . . . I hadn't thought about it that way, but I have six observations . . ." to which I might ask (sometimes seriously), "Only six?"

I am also grateful for the opportunity to share this work with you and hope that it opens gateways to Presence that will enhance your well-being.

NOTES

INTRODUCTION

xix **Research shows how powerful:** Patrick L. Hill and Nicholas A. Turiano, "Purpose in Life as a Predictor of Mortality Across Adulthood," *Psychological Science* 25, no. 7 (2014): 1482–1486; Stacey M. Schaefer, Jennifer Morozink Boylan, Carien M. van Reekum, Regina C. Lapate, Catherine J. Norris, Carol D. Ryff, and Richard J. Davidson, "Purpose in Life Predicts Better Emotional Recovery from Negative Stimuli," *PLOS One* 8, no. 11 (2013): 1–9; Carol Ryff, "Psychological Well-Being Revisited: Advances in Science and Practice," *Psychotherapy and Psychosomatics* 83, no. 1 (2014): 10–28.

xxii **Research confirms that being present:** Elissa S. Epel, Eli Puterman, Jue Lin, Elizabeth Blackburn, Alanie Lazaro, and Wendy Berry Mendes, "Wandering Minds and Aging Cells," *Clinical Psychological Science* 1, no. 1 (2012): 75–83.

PART 1 • THE POWER OF PRESENCE

1 **"We don't need to be perfect":** Mary Pipher, "Flourishing as We Age," keynote address at "Therapy in a Challenging World," Psychotherapy Networker Symposium, Washington, D.C., March 22, 2019.

1 **During our average day, most of us speak:** Susan David, *Emotional Agility: Get Unstuck, Embrace Change, and Thrive in Work and Life* (New York: Avery, 2015), 20.

3 **As Mark Twain said:** Fred Shapiro, "You Can Quote Them," *Yale Alumni Magazine*, September/October 2011, yalealumnimagazine .com/articles/3269-you-can-quote-them.

3 **I'll be using the terms** *Presence, mindfulness,* **and** *mindful awareness*: Jon Kabat-Zinn, *Mindfulness for Beginners: Reclaiming the Present Moment—and Your Life* (Boulder, CO: Sounds True, 2012), 1.

3 **Sometimes Kabat-Zinn adds the phrase:** Kabat-Zinn, *Mindfulness for Beginners*, 17.

3 **Mindfulness teacher Susan Bauer-Wu:** Susan Bauer-Wu, *Leaves Falling Gently: Living Fully with Serious and Life-Limiting Illness Through Mindfulness, Compassion, and Connectedness* (Oakland, CA: New Harbinger, 2011), 5.

5 **Psychologists Matthew Killingsworth and Daniel Gilbert studied:** M. A. Killingsworth and D. T. Gilbert, "A Wandering Mind Is an Unhappy Mind," *Science* 330, no. 6006 (2010): 932.

7 **These features are inspired by the work:** John Teasdale, Mark Williams, and Zindel Segal, *The Mindful Way Workbook: An 8-Week Program to Free Yourself from Depression and Emotional Distress* (New York: Guilford Press, 2014), 22–25.

9 **Teasdale, Williams, and Segal explain it this way:** Teasdale et al., *Mindful Way Workbook*, 65.

12 **Research professor Brené Brown uses the story:** Brené Brown, *Live Talks Los Angeles*, March 24, 2017.

13 **Exploring our challenges with kindness and curiosity:** Juliana G. Breines and Serena Chen, "Self-Compassion Increases Self-Improvement Motivation," *Personality and Social Psychology Bulletin* 38, no. 9 (2012): 1,133–1,143.

13 **We each experience aversion:** Elizabeth Blackburn and Elissa Epel, *The Telomere Effect: A Revolutionary Approach to Living Younger, Healthier, Longer* (New York: Grand Central, 2017), 149.

14 **Psychologist Shauna Shapiro:** Dr. Shauna Shapiro, *Mindfulness/ Heartfulness,* "Mind, Consciousness, and the Cultivation of Well-Being," Interpersonal Neurobiology Conference, UCLA, Los Angeles, California, March 3–5, 2017.

14 **Many mindfulness teachers use the phrase:** Teasdale et al., *Mindful Way Workbook,* 130.

16 **Author Byron Katie urges her students:** Byron Katie and Stephen Mitchell, *A Thousand Names for Joy: Living in Harmony with the Way Things Are* (New York: Three Rivers Press, 2008), x.

17 **UCLA researcher Susan Smalley and mindfulness teacher Diana Winston:** Susan Smalley and Diana Winston, *Fully Present: The Science, Art, and Practice of Mindfulness* (Boston: Da Capo Lifelong Books, 2010), 185–186.

17 **Meditation teacher Sharon Salzberg describes:** Sharon Salzberg, interview with the author, January 18, 2018.

20 **The science underlying the benefits of mindfulness:** Daniel Goleman and Richard J. Davidson, *Altered Traits: Science Reveals How Meditation Changes Your Mind, Brain, and Body* (New York: Avery, 2017), 14, 77.

21 **More good news: Our brain's ability to form:** Maddalena Boccia, Laura Piccardi, and Paola Guariglia, "The Meditative Mind: A Comprehensive Meta-Analysis of MRI Studies," *BioMed Research International* (2015), http://dx.doi.org/10.1155/2015/419808.

21 **Neuroscientist Carla Shatz has paraphrased researcher Donald Hebb's hypothesis:** Carla Shatz, "The Developing Brain," *Scientific American* 267, no. 3 (September 1992): 60–67.

22 **Here is the process as it relates to attention:** Daniel Siegel, *Aware: The Science and Practice of Presence—The Groundbreaking Meditation Practice* (New York: TarcherPerigee, 2018), 19.

22 **As Goleman and Davidson point out:** Goleman and Davidson, *Altered Traits,* 17.

22 **Neuroscientist Judson Brewer points out that while the exact functions:** Judson Brewer, *The Craving Mind: From Cigarettes to Smartphones to Love—Why We Get Hooked and How We Can Break Bad Habits* (New Haven, CT: Yale University Press, 2017), 100.

25 **Researcher Kristin Neff, a pioneer in the field, identifies three core components:** Filip Raes, Elizabeth Pommier, Kristin D. Neff, and Dinska Van Gucht, "Construction and Factorial Validation of a Short Form of the Self-Compassion Scale," *Clinical Psychology and Psychotherapy* 18, no. 3 (2011): 250–255; Kristin D. Neff and Katie A. Dahm, "Self-Compassion: What It Is, What It Does, and How It Relates to Mindfulness," in *Mindfulness and Self-Regulation*, eds. Brian D. Ostafin, Michael D. Robinson, and Brian P. Meier (New York: Springer, 2015), 121–137; Kristin Neff, "Self-Compassion: An Alternative Conceptualization of a Healthy Attitude Toward Oneself," *Self and Identity* 2: 85–101.

26 **Neff has experienced the power of self-compassion:** Kristin Neff, Interpersonal Neurobiology Conference, UCLA, Los Angeles, California, March 17–19, 2017.

26 **Self-compassion is about being kind:** Neff, Interpersonal Neurobiology Conference, UCLA, Los Angeles, California, March 17–19, 2017.

26 **Research shows that 80 percent of us:** Karen Bluth, "How to Help Teens Become More Self-Compassionate," *Greater Good Magazine*, October 19, 2017, https://greatergood.berkeley.edu/article/item/how_to_help_teens_become_more_self_compassionate.

26 **People who practice self-compassion enjoy myriad:** Amy L. Finlay-Jones, Clare S. Rees, and Robert T. Kane, "Self-Compassion, Emotion Regulation and Stress Among Australian Psychologists: Testing an Emotion Regulation Model of Self-Compassion Using Structural Equation Modeling," *PLOS One* 10, no. 7 (July 2015): e0133481.

26 **As Neff points out, increased self-compassion:** Kristin Neff, "Mind, Consciousness, and the Cultivation of Well-Being," Interpersonal Neurobiology Conference, UCLA, Los Angeles, California, March 8, 2017.

27 **One study of divorced couples:** David A. Sbarra, Hillary L. Smith, and Matthias R. Mehl, "When Leaving Your Ex, Love Yourself: Observational Ratings of Self-Compassion Predict the Course of Emotional Recovery Following Marital Separation," *Psychological Science* 23, no. 3 (August 2011): 261–269.

27 **Similarly, for veterans just back from combat:** Regina Hiraoka, Eric C. Meyer, Nathan A. Kimbrel, Bryann B. DeBeer, Suzy Bird Gulliver, and Sandra B. Morissette, "Self-Compassion as a Prospective Predictor of PTSD Symptom Severity Among Trauma-Exposed U.S. Iraq and Afghanistan War Veterans," *Journal of Traumatic Stress* 28, no. 2 (April 2015): 127–133.

27 **"Perfection doesn't make you feel perfect . . .":** Maria Shriver, *I've Been Thinking . . . : Reflections, Prayers, and Meditations for a Meaningful Life* (New York: Pamela/Dorman Books, 2018), 75.

28 **Self-Compassion Scale—Short Form:** https://self-compassion.org /wp-content/uploads/2015/02/ShortSCS.pdf

29 **You may be aware that psychologists extolled:** Kristin Neff, Interpersonal Neurobiology Conference, UCLA, Los Angeles, California, March 17–19, 2017.

33 **Brewer calls the brain:** Judson Brewer and Tara Healey, "How the Science and Practice of Awareness Supports Well-Being and Performance," workshop at the Mindful Life Conference, Arlington, Virginia, April 28, 2016.

34 **Research psychologist Ellen Langer explains:** Amanda Ie, Christelle T. Ngnoumen, and Ellen J. Langer, *The Wiley Blackwell Handbook of Mindfulness* (Hoboken, NJ: Wiley, 2014), 11–26.

34 **Part of our eagerness to always fill in:** Jennifer J. Freyd, "Five Hunches About Perceptual Processes and Dynamic Representations," in *Attention and Performance XIV: Synergies in Experimental Psychology, Artificial Intelligence, and Cognitive Neuroscience*, eds. David E. Meyer and Sylvan Kornblum (Cambridge, MA: MIT Press, 1993), 99–119.

35 **Langer's research shows that when:** Ie et al., *The Wiley Blackwell Handbook of Mindfulness*, 11–26.

35 **Nothing lasts, nothing is finished:** Richard Powell, *Wabi-Sabi Simple: Create Beauty. Value Imperfection. Live Deeply* (Avon, MA: Adams Media, 2004).

36 **Male students consistently overestimate their grade point average (GPA):** Tara Sophia Mohr, "Why Women Don't Apply for Jobs Unless They're 100% Qualified," *Harvard Business Review*, August 25, 2014, https://hbr.org/2014/08/why-women-dont -apply-for-jobs-unless-theyre-100-qualified.

37 **Furthermore, upon finding jobs, nearly 60 percent of men:** Sheryl Sandberg, "Why We Women Have Too Few Women Leaders," filmed 2010 in Washington, D.C., TEDWomen video, 14:51, https://www.ted.com/talks/sheryl_sandberg_why_we_have_too _few_women_leaders/up-next?language=en.

40 **Neuroscientist Amishi Jha grew up in India:** Amishi Jha, interview with the author, November 8, 2017.

40 **As director of her science lab:** Amishi Jha, interview with the author, November 8, 2017.

41 **"I think that being here is it":** John O'Donohue and Daniel J. Siegel, "Awakening the Mind," workshop, the Berkshires, Massachusetts, 2006, cited in Daniel J. Siegel, *Aware: The Science and Practice of Presence* (New York: TarcherPerigee, 2018), 347.

44 **Research shows that women have higher stress levels:** "Stress in America™: The State of Our Nation," annual survey, American Psychological Association, 2017, https://www.apa.org/news/press /releases/stress/2017/state-nation.pdf.

44 **What changed McGonigal's mind about stress:** Kelly McGonigal, *The Upside of Stress: Why Stress Is Good for You, and How to Get Good at It* (New York: Avery, 2016), 2–3.

45 **McGonigal explains it this way:** McGonigal, *Upside of Stress*, 87.

45 **Staying in a threat state for long periods:** Carol S. Dweck, *Mindset: The New Psychology of Success* (New York: Ballantine, 2006).

46 **Social scientists use what's called *minority stress theory*:** Elizabeth Grace Holman, "Theoretical Extensions of Minority Stress Theory for Sexual Minority Individuals in the Workplace: A Cross-Contextual Understanding of Minority Stress Processes," *Journal of Family Theory* 10, no. 1 (2018); Dorainne J. Levy, Jennifer A. Heissel, Jennifer A. Richeson, and Emma K. Adam, "Psychological and Biological Responses to Race-Based Social Stress as Pathways to Disparities in Educational Outcomes," *American Psychologist* 71, no. 6 (2016): 455–473; David M. Frost, Keren Lehavot, Ilan H. Meyer, "Minority Stress and Physical Health Among Sexual Minority Individuals," *Journal of Behaviorial Medicine* 38, no. 1 (2015): 1–8; Ilan H. Meyer, "Prejudice, Social Stress, and Mental Health in Lesbian, Gay, and Bisexual Populations: Conceptual Issues and Research Evidence," *Psychological Bulletin* 129, no. 5 (2003): 19.

46 **Women with children struggle to adapt their careers:** Julie Creswell, "As PepsiCo's CEO Plans Exit, Women's Corporate Clout Fades," *Star Business Journal*, August 7, 2018, https://www .businessbreakingnews.net/2018/08/as-pepsicos-ceo-plans-exit -womens-corporate-clout-fades/.

47 **When I asked Jacqueline about the motherhood penalty:** Jacqueline Carter, interview with the author, July 25, 2018.

47 **Business leaders espouse "family-friendly" values:** Emma Jacobs, "Personal Photos at Work: Pictures That Paint a Thousand Words," *Financial Times*, August 17, 2015, https://www.ft.com /content/e4a39190-39f8-11e5-bbd1-b37bc06f590c.

48 **Generally, employers have been seen rewarding fathers:** Jacobs, "Personal Photos at Work."

48 **Studies of heterosexual couples confirm:** Melanie E. Brewster, "Lesbian Women and Household Labor Division: A Systematic Review of Scholarly Research from 2000 to 2015," *Journal of Lesbian Studies* 21, no. 1 (September 2016): 47–69; Samantha L. Tornello, Bettina N. Sonnenberg, and Charlotte J. Patterson, "Division of Labor Among Gay Fathers: Associations with Parent, Couple, and Child Adjustment," *Psychology of Sexual Orientation and Gender Diversity* 2, no. 4 (2015): 365–375; Charlotte J. Patterson, Erin L. Sutfin, and Megan Fulcher, "Division of Labor Among Lesbian and Heterosexual Parenting Couples: Correlates of Specialized Versus Shared Patterns," *Journal of Adult Development* 11, no. 3 (July 2004): 179–189.

48 **Research on other groups in the LGBTQ+ community:** Carla A. Pfeffer, "Women's Work? Women Partners of Transgender Men Doing Housework and Emotion Work," *Journal of Marriage and Family* 72, no. 1 (January 2010): 165–183.

48 **Research has also found that mothers' paid work hours:** Annette Lareau and Elliot B. Weininger, "Time, Work, and Family Life: Reconceptualizing Gendered Time Patterns Through the Case of Children's Organized Activities," *Sociological Forum* 23, no. 3 (September 2008); Judith Shulevitz, "Mom: The Designated Worrier," *New York Times*, May 8, 2015, SR1.

48 **Respondents in one study said:** Elizabeth J. McClean, Sean R. Martin, Kyle J. Emich, and Todd Woodruff, "The Social Consequences of Voice: An Examination of Voice Type and Gender on Status and Subsequent Leader Emergence," *Academy of*

Management Journal 61, no. 5 (October 2018); Heather Murphy, "Picture a Leader. Is She a Woman?" *New York Times*, March 16, 2018, A1.

49 **When Anne-Marie Slaughter first became the dean:** Anne-Marie Slaughter, "Why Women Still Can't Have It All," *The Atlantic*, July 2012, https://www.theatlantic.com/magazine/archive/2012/07/why -women-still-cant-have-it-all/309020/.

50 **One does not practice meditation:** Elizabeth Lesser, *The Seeker's Guide: Making Your Life a Spiritual Adventure* (New York: Villard, 2000), 97.

50 **As psychologist Daniel Goleman and neuroscientist Richard Davidson:** Goleman and Davidson, *Altered Traits*, 74.

52 **What I remind myself on such days:** Trudy Goodman, interview with the author, February 20, 2018.

53 **This may be the number one excuse:** Goleman and Davidson, *Altered Traits*, 276.

53 **mindfulness teacher Sharon Salzberg,:** Sharon Salzberg, interview with the author, January 18, 2018.

54 **As Jon Kabat-Zinn says:** Jon Kabat-Zinn, "Creating Connections III," Resilience Through Connection Conference, Efteling, Netherlands, April 16, 2015.

56 **there are many different types of meditation practices:** Antoine Lutz, Heleen A. Slagter, and Richard J. Davidson, "Attention Regulation and Monitoring in Meditation," *Trends in Cognitive Sciences* 12, no. 4 (2008): 163–169.

57 **Poet Diane Ackerman does what she calls:** Diane Ackerman, interview with the author, January 23, 2017.

58 **In a third type of mindfulness meditation, compassion:** David R. Vago and David A. Silbersweig, "Self-Awareness, Self-Regulation, and Self-Transcendence (S-ART): A Framework for Understanding

the Neurobiological Mechanisms of Mindfulness," *Frontiers in Human Neuroscience* 6 (October 2012): 296.

58 **Lovingkindness meditation has been associated:** Barbara L. Fredrickson, Michael A. Cohn, Kimberly A. Coffey, Jolynn Pek, and Sandra M. Finkel, "Open Hearts Build Lives: Positive Emotions, Induced Through Loving-Kindness Meditation, Build Consequential Personal Resources," *Journal of Personality and Social Psychology* 95, no. 5 (August 2011): 1045–1062; Cendri A. Hutcherson, Emma Seppala, and James J. Gross, "The Neural Correlates of Social Connection," *Cognitive, Affective, and Behavioral Neuroscience* 15, no. 1 (July 2014): 1–14.

58 **Research has also shown that meditation incorporating:** Goleman and Davidson, *Altered Traits*.

59 **One student put it this way:** Anonymous, yoga class, 1440 Multiversity, Scotts Valley, California, December 11, 2017.

59 **Similarly, mindfulness leader Sharon Salzberg reminds us:** Sharon Salzberg, interview with the author, January 18, 2018.

59 **Anxiety and stress have sometimes been correlated:** Goleman and Davidson, *Altered Traits*, 87–88.

60 **With focused attention training:** Siegel, *Aware*.

62 **A recent study by research psychologist Lawrence Barsalou:** Lawrence Barsalou, unpublished research presented at the Mind and Life Summer Institute, Garrison Institute, New York, New York, June 9, 2019.

63 **Enacting behaviors to reduce suffering:** Helen Riess with Liz Neporent, *The Empathy Effect: Seven Neuroscience-Based Keys for Transforming the Way We Live, Love, Work, and Connect Across Differences* (Boulder, CO: Sounds True, 2018). Paul Gilbert points out in *The Compassionate Mind: A New Approach to Life's Challenges* (Oakland, CA: New Harbinger, 2010) that cultivating empathy

and compassion enables us to *be present* and remain receptive without becoming reactive. Sometimes just bearing witness to suffering—in other words, being open to another's pain with care and concern—helps reduce isolation, and in that way soothes the sufferer.

64 **Two scientists, Elissa Epel and Nobel Prize winner Elizabeth Blackburn:** Blackburn and Epel, *The Telomere Effect*, 76.

65 **They also found the more stressed out the mothers felt:** Blackburn and Epel, *The Telomere Effect*, 76.

65 **Work stress is not related to shorter telomeres:** Elissa Epel, "Cultivating Stress Resilience: The Science of Renewal," lecture, 1440 Multiversity, Scotts Valley, California, April 20, 2018.

66 **Another way of assessing both functional and structural integration:** Siegel, *Aware*.

67 **Addiction involves fluctuations of dopamine levels:** Judson Brewer, *The Craving Mind*.

70 **Research scientist Sará King studies the experiences of urban youth:** Sará King, interview with the author, June 2, 2019.

71 **London-based Razeea Lemaignen, health and well-being consultant:** Razeea Lemaignen, interview with the author, November 11, 2017.

74 **Gretchen Rubin, author and self-proclaimed "happiness bully":** Gretchen Rubin, *The Four Tendencies: The Indispensable Personality Profiles That Reveal How to Make Your Life Better (and Other People's Lives Better, Too)* (New York: Harmony Books, 2017).

75 **Blackburn practices what she calls *micro-meditations*:** Blackburn and Epel, *The Telomere Effect*, 113.

77 **Mindfulness leader Sharon Salzberg advises:** Sharon Salzberg, interview with the author, January 18, 2018.

77 **Researchers at the University of Wisconsin:** Goleman and Davidson, *Altered Traits*, 76.

77–78 **Tips for Getting Started with Your MAPP:** Blackburn and Epel, *The Telomere Effect*, 76.

84–85 **Quieting the Inner Critic:** Adapted with permission from Sharon Salzberg, *Real Happiness: The Power of Meditation* (New York: Workman, 2011), 163–164.

PART 2 · PRESENCE AND PURPOSE

88 **As Sanjiv Chopra and Gina Vild explain:** Sanjiv Chopra and Gina Vild, *The Two Most Important Days: How to Find Your Purpose— and Live a Happier, Healthier Life* (New York: Thomas Dunne, 2017), 9–10.

88 **On the other hand, if what we value and work toward:** Barbara Bradley Hagerty, *Life Reimagined: The Science, Art, and Opportunity of Midlife* (New York: Riverhead Books, 2017), 133.

88 **Purpose researcher William Damon:** William Damon, *The Path to Purpose: How Young People Find Their Calling in Life* (New York: First Free Press, 2009), 31.

88 **Happiness is a choice:** Chopra and Vild, *The Two Most Important Days*, 10.

89 **Here's an example of Purpose from behavior scientist:** Victor J. Strecher, *Life on Purpose: How Living for What Matters Most Changes Everything* (San Francisco: HarperOne, 2016), 11.

89 **Let's start with the definition that is commonly used:** Patrick E. McKnight and Todd B. Kashdan, "Purpose in Life as a System That Creates and Sustains Health and Well-Being: An Integrative, Testable Theory," *Review of General Psychology* 13, no. 3 (September 2009): 242–251.

89 **Damon explains that our Purpose:** Damon, *The Path to Purpose*, 44.

90 **As Damon puts it, "Often it is the people":** Damon, *The Path to Purpose*, 20.

90 **Damon's definition of purpose makes clear:** Damon, *The Path to Purpose*, 33.

91 **Purpose refers to having direction and is more goal oriented:** Frank Martela and Michael F. Steger, "The Three Meanings of Meaning in Life: Distinguishing Coherence, Purpose, and Significance," *Journal of Positive Psychology* 11, no. 5 (2016): 532; Samantha Heintzelman and Laura A. King, "Life Is Pretty Meaningful," *American Psychologist* 69, no. 6 (September 2014): 561–574.

92 **Researchers Frank Martela and Michael Steger describe it this way:** Martela and Steger, "The Three Meanings of Meaning in Life," 534.

92 **Presence and Purpose can center us when our expectations aren't met:** Cortland J. Dahl and Richard J. Davidson, "Mindfulness and the Contemplative Life: Pathways to Connection, Insight, and Purpose," *Current Opinion in Psychology* 28 (August 2019): 60–64.

92 **Within the psychology literature on Purpose or meaning:** Kendall Cotton Bronk, Patrick L. Hill, Daniel K. Lapsley, Tasneem L. Talib, and Holmes Finch, "Purpose, Hope, and Life Satisfaction in Three Age Groups," *Journal of Positive Psychology* 4, no. 6 (2009): 500–510.

93 **Not surprisingly, studies confirm that *high levels*:** Michael F. Steger, Patricia A. Frazier, Matthew Kaler, and Shigehiro Oishi, "The Meaning in Life Questionnaire: Assessing the Presence of and Search for Meaning in Life," *Journal of Counseling Psychology* 53, no. 1 (2006): 80–93; Michael F. Steger, Todd B. Kashdan, Brandon A. Sullivan, and Danielle Lorentz, "Understanding the Search for Meaning in Life: Personality, Cognitive Style, and the Dynamic Between Seeking and Experiencing Meaning," *Journal of Personality* 76, no. 2 (May 2008): 199–228; Michael Steger, Joshua R.

Mann, Phil Michels, and Tyler C. Cooper, "Meaning in Life, Anxiety, Depression, and General Health Among Smoking Cessation Patients," *Journal of Psychosomatic Research* 67, no. 4 (October 2009): 353–358.

93 **One study of "9-enders":** Adam L. Alter and Hal E. Hershfield, "People Search for Meaning When They Approach a New Decade in Chronological Age," *Proceedings of the National Academy of Sciences* 111, no. 48 (December 2014): 17066–17070.

95 **As Steve Jobs said, "You can't connect the dots . . .":** Steve Jobs, "'You've Got to Find What You Love,' Jobs Says," *Stanford News*, June 12, 2005, https://news.stanford.edu/2005/06/14 /jobs-061505/.

98 **Furthermore, as journalist Barbara Hagerty points out:** Hagerty, *Life Reimagined*, 7.

98 **And no matter our age, with Purpose:** Stacey M. Schaefer, Jennifer Morozink Boylan, Carien M. van Reekum, Regina C. Lapate, Catherine J. Norris, Carol D. Ryff, and Richard J. Davidson, "Purpose in Life Predicts Better Emotional Recovery from Negative Stimuli," *PLOS One* 8, no. 11 (November 2013): 1–9.

98 **A study at the University of Michigan Health System:** Jane Dutton, Gelaye Debebe, and Amy Wrzesniewski, "Being Valued and Devalued at Work: A Social Valuing Perspective," *Qualitative Organizational Research: Best Papers from the Davis Conference on Qualitative Research* no. 3 (2012).

99 **When I asked Rhonda Magee:** Rhonda Magee, interview with the author, July 8, 2019.

99 **In addressing organizations around the United States:** Rhonda Magee, interview with the author, July 8, 2019.

101 **I'll be dispelling three of the most common myths:** Heather Malin, *Teaching for Purpose: Preparing Students for Lives of*

Meaning (Cambridge, MA: Harvard Education Press, 2018), 30.

102 **Innovators Bill Burnett and Dave Evans found:** Bill Burnett and Dave Evans, *Designing Your Life: How to Build a Well-Lived, Joyful Life* (New York: Knopf, 2016), xxix.

102 **Malin explains that although it's great if our Purpose:** Heather Malin, *Teaching for Purpose: Preparing Students for Lives of Meaning* (Cambridge, MA: Harvard Education Press, 2018), 30.

102 **Nonetheless, it is in the nature of Purpose:** Damon, *Path to Purpose*, 34.

103 **Malin puts it this way:** Malin, *Teaching for Purpose*, 31.

103 **The World Values Survey, a global research project:** Ron Inglehart et al. (eds.), "World Values Survey: Round Six—Country-Pooled Datafile Version," 2014, http://www.world valuessurvey.org/WVSDocumentationWV6.jsp.

104 **That's how it worked out for Peggy O'Kane:** Peggy O'Kane, interview with the author, October 17, 2017.

104 **Marie Tsuruda, a gentle, soft-spoken, second-generation Japanese American:** Marie Tsuruda, interview with the author, June 2, 2017.

106 **Palliative care nurse Bronnie Ware identified these top five regrets:** Bronnie Ware, *The Top Five Regrets of the Dying: A Life Transformed by the Dearly Departing* (Carlsbad, CA: Hay House, 2012).

106 **Michelle Obama had the following thoughts about Barack:** Michelle Obama, *Becoming* (New York: Crown, 2018), 131–132.

107 **Around this same time, Michelle realized the following:** Obama, *Becoming*, 132.

107 **Bronnie Ware summarizes the value of friends this way:** Ware, *The Top Five Regrets of the Dying*, 231.

108 **Loneliness is more harmful to:** Brené Brown, *Rising Strong: How the Ability to Reset Transforms the Way We Live, Love, Parent, and Lead* (New York: Random House, 2017).

108 **In fact, *not having strong social connections*:** Julianne Holt-Lunstad, Timothy B. Smith, and J. Bradley Layton, "Social Relationships and Mortality Risk: A Meta-Analytic Review," *PLOS Medicine* 7, no. 7 (2010): 14–15; Julianne Holt-Lunstad, Timothy B. Smith, Mark Baker, Tyler Harris, and David Stephenson, "Loneliness and Social Isolation as Risk Factors for Mortality: A Meta-Analytic Review," *Perspectives on Psychological Science* 10, no. 2 (2015): 227–237.

109 **Mindfulness teacher Sharon Salzberg cautions:** Sharon Salzberg, interview with the author, January 18, 2018.

110 **As Zen priest Joan Halifax says in *Standing at the Edge:*** Joan Halifax, *Standing at the Edge: Finding Freedom Where Fear and Courage Meet* (New York: Flatiron Books, 2018), 195–196.

111 **When it comes to sleep, for example, research shows:** Rasmus Hougaard and Jacqueline Carter, "Senior Executives Get More Sleep Than Everyone Else," *Harvard Business Review*, February 28, 2018, https://hbr.org/2018/02/senior-executives-get-more-sleep -than-everyone-else.

111 **MIT professor Sherry Turkle has spent her life studying:** Sherry Turkle, *Alone Together: Why We Expect More from Technology and Less from Each Other* (New York: Basic Books, 2012).

111 **Research supports a link between social media:** Jenna L. Clark, Sara B. Algoe, and Melanie C. Green, "Social Network Sites and Well-Being: The Role of Social Connection," *Current Directions in Psychological Science* 27, no. 1 (2018): 32–37.

112 **Women are more likely than men to become addicted:** Cecilie Schou Andreassen, Joël Billieux, Mark D. Griffiths, Daria J. Kuss, Zsolt Demetrovics, Elvis Mazzoni, and Ståle Pallesen, "The Relationship Between Addictive Use of Social Media and Video Games and Symptoms of Psychiatric Disorders: A Large-Scale Cross-Sectional Study," *Psychology of Addictive Behaviors* 30, no. 2 (2016): 252–262.

113 **Our brains have literally become addicted:** Regina J.J.M. van den Eijnden, Jeroen S. Lemmens, and Patti M. Valkenburg, "The Social Media Disorder Scale," *Science Direct* 61 (August 2016): 478-487.

114 **In one research study that illustrates how:** Sarah F. Brosnan and Frans B. M. de Waal, "Monkeys Reject Unequal Pay," *Nature* 425, no. 6955 (2003): 297–299.

115 **Not surprisingly, researchers found a link between depression:** Mai-Ly N. Steers, Robert E. Wickham, and Linda K. Acitelli, "Seeing Everyone Else's Highlight Reels: How Facebook Usage Is Linked to Depressive Symptoms," *Journal of Social and Clinical Psychology* 33, no. 8 (2014): 701–731.

117 **As Diane Ackerman puts it:** http://www.dianeackerman.com/home.

117 **If we don't honor integration, we may experience chaos or rigidity:** Daniel J. Siegel, *Mind: A Journey to the Heart of Being Human* (New York: W. W. Norton, 2017).

118 **As the Dalai Lama reminds us, "Gratitude helps us catalog":** His Holiness the Dalai Lama and Archbishop Desmond Tutu, with Douglas Abrams, *The Book of Joy: Lasting Happiness in a Changing World* (New York: Avery, 2016), 249.

118 **Purpose researcher William Damon expresses:** Damon, *The Path to Purpose*, 141.

118 **Studies show that gratitude is strongly and consistently correlated:** "In Praise of Gratitude," Harvard Mental Health

Letter, November 2011, https://www.health.harvard.edu/newsletter
_article/in-praise-of-gratitude.

119 **A recent study divided participants into three groups:** Robert A.
Emmons and Michael E. McCullough, "Counting Blessings
Versus Burdens: An Experimental Investigation of Gratitude and
Subjective Well-Being in Daily Life," *Journal of Personality and
Social Psychology* 84, no. 2 (2016): 377–389.

120 **In one study, a test group of psychotherapy clients was
instructed:** Y. Joel Wong, Jesse Owen, Nicole T. Gabana, Joshua W.
Brown, Sydney McInnis, Paul Toth, and Lynn Gilman,
"Does Gratitude Writing Improve the Mental Health of
Psychotherapy Clients? Evidence from a Randomized
Controlled Trial," *Psychotherapy Research* 28, no. 2 (2018):
192–202.

123 **Similarly, studies show that women may be reluctant:** Tara Sophia
Mohr, "Why Women Don't Apply for Jobs Unless They're 100%
Qualified," *Harvard Business Review*, August 25, 2014, https://hbr
.org/2014/08/why-women-dont-apply-for-jobs-unless
-theyre-100-qualified.

123 **A thirty- to fifty-year-old woman in the United States today:**
Social Security Administration, "Retirement & Survivors Benefits:
Life Expectancy Calculator," https://www.ssa.gov/OACT/population
/longevity.html.

124 **Research suggests that volunteering slows the cognitive
decline:** Demetria Gallegos, "Research Finds Volunteering
Can Be Good for Your Health," *Wall Street Journal*, April 22,
2018.

124 **Research suggests that volunteering for unselfish reasons:** Sara
Konrath, Andrea Fuhrel-Forbis, Alina Lou, and Stephanie Brown,
"Motives for Volunteering Are Associated with Mortality Risk in
Older Adults," *Health Psychology* 31, no. 1 (2012): 87, cited in
Hagerty, 300n40.

124 **Research confirms that generative people are healthier:** Dan P. McAdams, "Generativity in Midlife," in Margie E. Lachman, *Handbook of Midlife Development* (New York: Wiley, 2001), 295–443; Dan P. McAdams and Jen Guo, "Narrating the Generative Life," *Psychological Science* 26, no. 4 (2015): 475–483.

125 **Those of you familiar with Dan Siegel's work:** Daniel J. Siegel, *Aware: The Science and Practice of Presence* (New York: TarcherPerigee, 2018), 249.

128 **Below is the 3-Minute Breathing Space:** John Teasdale, Mark Williams, and Zindel Segal, *The Mindful Way Workbook: An 8-Week Program to Free Yourself from Depression and Emotional Distress* (New York: Guilford Press, 2014), 208.

PART 3 · PRESENCE AND PIVOTING

131 **"Don't ever make decisions based on fear":** Michelle Obama, *Becoming* (New York: Crown, 2018).

133 **Indra Nooyi, former chair and CEO of PepsiCo:** Julie Creswell, "Indra Nooyi, PepsiCo C.E.O. Who Pushed for Healthier Products, to Step Down," *The New York Times*, August 6, 2018, https://www.nytimes.com/2018/08/06/business/indra-nooyi-pepsi.html.

139 **Rich Fernandez, CEO of Search Inside Yourself Leadership Institute:** Rich Fernandez and Laura Delizonna, "Thriving at Work with Mindfulness," workshop at Mindful Life Conference, Arlington, Virginia, April 28, 2016.

141 **Sky Jarrett, a self-proclaimed "recovering, overachieving perfectionist":** Sky Jarrett, interview with the author, June 4, 2018.

142 **Our negative brains can easily conjure up:** Rick Hanson, *Buddha's Brain: The Practical Neuroscience of Happiness, Love, and Wisdom* (Oakland, CA: New Harbinger, 2009).

143 **The following question was posed in a room:** Eric Schmidt and Jonathan Rosenberg, *How Google Works* (New York: Grand Central, 2017); Susan Chira, "Why Women Aren't CEOs, According to the Women Who Almost Were," *New York Times*, July 23, 2017, https://www.nytimes.com/2017/07/21/sunday-review/women-ceos-glass-ceiling.html.

145 **I noticed the following inscription:** Kameelah Janan Rasheed is the Brooklyn Library's 2019 Radin Artist-in-Residence, https://www.artforum.com/interviews/kameelah-janan-rasheed-talks-about-her-work-at-the-brooklyn-public-library-79129.

145 **Building on the work of psychologists Amos Tversky and Daniel Kahneman:** Daniel Kahneman won the Nobel Prize in economics science in 2002 for his research with Amos Tversky on prospect theory from 1971 to 1979 (Tversky was deceased by the time the Nobel was awarded). Erica Goode, "A Conversation with Daniel Kahneman; On Profit, Loss and the Mysteries of the Mind," *New York Times*, November 5, 2002, https://www.nytimes.com/2002/11/05/health/a-conversation-with-daniel-kahneman-on-profit-loss-and-the-mysteries-of-the-mind.html; Sabrina M. Tom, Craig R. Fox, Christopher Trepel, and Russell A. Poldrack, "The Neural Basis of Loss Aversion in Decision-Making under Risk," *Science* 315, no. 5811 (2007): 515–518.

161 **Similarly, Apple, Oracle, Intuit, Udemy, GoDaddy, Campbell Soup, and many:** Claire Zillman, "Apple Joins Growing Crop of Tech Firms Offering 'Returnships' to Moms Who Left the Workplace," *Fortune*, November 28, 2017.

161 **As iRelaunch founders Carol Fishman Cohen and Vivian Steir Rabin put it:** "The Advocate for the 40-Year-Old Interns: iRelaunch CEO Carol Fishman Cohen," *The—M—Dash*, April 21, 2017, https://mmlafleur.com/mdash/carol-fishman-cohen-irelaunch.

161 **Other useful programs for those getting back on the career track:** See Lean In, https://leanincircles.org/chapter/return-to-work, and ReBootAccel, https://rebootaccel.com.

162 **In the mid-1700s, Jeanne Baret became the first woman:** Ailsa Ross, "The Insouciant Heiress Who Became the First Western Woman to Enter Palmyra," *Atlas Obscura*, February 10, 2016, https://www.atlasobscura.com/articles/the-insouciant-heiress -who-became-the-first-western-woman-to-enter-palmyra.

162 **Nellie Bly, an American journalist in the late 1800s:** Rosemary J. Brown, "Top 10 Inspiring Female Adventurers," *The Guardian*, March 8, 2016.

163 **"More reliably than anything else on earth":** Gloria Steinem, *My Life on the Road* (New York: Random House, 2016), xxiii.

165 **Salzberg describes the benefit of mini-meditations:** Sharon Salzberg, *Real Happiness: The Power of Meditation* (New York: Workman, 2011), 56.

166–167 **Visualization Practice for Pivoting:** Adapted with permission from Signe Simon, PhD, and Simone Humphrey, PhD, at LOVELINK.co.

PART 4 · PRESENCE AND PACING

169 **"A long view of time":** Krista Tippett, *Becoming Wise: An Inquiry into the Mystery and Art of Living* (New York: Penguin Press, 2016), 12.

171 **"If I Could Live My Life Over":** Nadine Stair, Essay. Nadine Stair purportedly wrote this essay decades ago while she was 85 years of age and residing in Louisville, Kentucky. Nothing else is presently known about the author. The essay appears to have been inspired by a 1953 work by Don Herold (1889–1966) titled "I'd Pick More Daisies," which in turn may have been inspired by an essay by Jorge Luis Borges (1899–1986) titled "Moments." A similar and more recent essay, also titled "If I Had My Life to Live Over," was written by Erma Louise Bombeck (1927–1996).

173 **My law school class was 50 percent women:** Mark DeWolf, "12 Stats About Working Women," *U.S. Department of Labor Blog*, March 1, 2017, https://blog.dol.gov/2017/03/01/12-stats-about -working-women.

173 **As Amy Westervelt, journalist and cohost of the *Range* podcast, puts it:** Amy Westervelt, "Having It All Kinda Sucks," *Huffington Post*, February 15, 2016, https://www.huffpost .com/entry/having-it-all-kinda-sucks_b_9237772.

173 **Westervelt is likely alluding to the controversial debate:** Sheryl Sandberg, *Lean In: Women, Work, and the Will to Lead* (New York: Knopf, 2013).

173 **A couple of years later, after the tragic passing of her husband:** Sheryl Sandberg and Adam Grant, *Option B: Facing Adversity, Building Resilience, and Finding Joy* (New York: Knopf, 2017), 71–72.

176 **Slaughter lamented that she frequently gets reactions:** Anne-Marie Slaughter, "Why Women Still Can't Have It All," *The Atlantic*, July/August 2012, https://www.theatlantic.com/magazine /archive/2012/07/why-women-still-cant-have-it-all/309020/.

181 **Studies show, for example, that 84 percent of executives:** Korn Ferry International Survey, 2014, https://www.kornferry.com/press /15179.

181 **And it turns out that making space *throughout*:** Ferris Jabr, "Why Your Brain Needs More Downtime," *Scientific American*, October 15, 2013, https://www.scientificamerican.com/article/mental -downtime/.

183 **Thoreau said, "Part of us awakes which slumbers . . .":** Henry David Thoreau, *Walden* (New York: Signet Classics, 2012), chap. 2.

187 **Alex Soojung-Kim Pang, founder of the Restful Company:** Alex Soojung-Kim Pang, *Rest: Why You Get More Done When You Work Less* (New York: Basic Books, 2018), 246–247.

187 **Pang recognizes that rest is often mistaken for idleness:** Pang, *Rest*, 247.

187 **Here's a story about rest from the German writer Heinrich Böll:** Brian O'Connor, "Why Doing Nothing Is One of the Most Important Things You Can Do," *Time*, June 15, 2018, https://time .com/5300633/doing-nothing-work-vacation-time-history-leisure/.

188 **Sociologist Christine Carter explains that we aren't taught to say no:** Christine Carter, *The Sweet Spot: How to Find Your Groove at Home and Work* (New York: Ballantine Books, 2015), 83.

188 **Mary Pipher said that the first time she said no:** Mary Pipher, "Flourishing as We Age," keynote address at "Therapy in a Challenging World," Psychotherapy Networker Symposium, Washington, D.C., March 22, 2019.

188 **A few months later when I asked Sue how it was going:** Sue Siegel, interview with the author, August 18, 2018.

190 **Sociologist Christine Carter, author of *The Sweet Spot* and *Raising Happiness*:** Carter, *The Sweet Spot*; Christine Carter, *Raising Happiness: 10 Simple Steps for More Joyful Kids and Happier Parents* (New York: Ballantine Books, 2010).

191 **It means that the brain doesn't multitask:** Daniel Goleman and Richard J. Davidson, *Altered Traits: Science Reveals How Meditation Changes Your Mind, Brain, and Body* (New York: Avery, 2017), 137.

192 **Computer scientist Cal Newport distinguishes what he calls:** Shankar Vedantam, "Hidden Brain: Researchers Delve into Improving Concentration," NPR, January 25, 2018, https://www .npr.org/2018/01/25/580577161/hidden-brain-researchers-delve -into-improving-concentration.

193 **Newport recommends scheduling time:** Cal Newport, *Deep Work: Rules for Focused Success in a Distracted World* (New York: Grand Central, 2016).

193 **Studies show, for example, that as soon as one:** Varoth Chotpitayasunondh and Karen M. Douglas, "How 'Phubbing' Becomes the Norm: The Antecedents and Consequences of Snubbing via Smartphone," *Computers in Human Behavior* 63 (October 2016): 9–18.

194 **Gopi Kallayil at Google is a leading voice:** Gopi Kallayil and Pico Iyer, "The Art of Stillness in the Digital Age," Wisdom 2.0 Conference, San Francisco, February 27–March 1, 2015.

194 **One study on such workplaces found that establishing:** Erin Reid and Lakshmi Ramarajan, "Managing the High-Intensity Workplace," *Harvard Business Review*, June 2016, https://hbr.org /2016/06/managing-the-high-intensity-workplace.

194 **Some countries are not leaving it to businesses:** David Z. Morris, "New French Law Bars Work Email After Hours," *Fortune*, January 1, 2017, https://fortune.com/2017/01/01/french-right -to-disconnect-law/.

194 **Many U.S. schools have issued policies to regulate:** Tovia Smith, "A School's Way to Fight Phones in Class: Lock 'Em Up," NPR, January 11, 2018, https://www.npr.org/2018/01/11 /577101803/a-schools-way-to-fight-phones-in-class-lock-em-up.

194 **France recently passed a law banning students:** Sam Schechner, "France Bans Phones for Children at School," *Wall Street Journal*, August 14, 2018, A1.

195 *Inner-net* **is a term coined by Kallayil:** Gopi Kallayil, *The Internet to the Inner-Net: Five Ways to Reset Your Connection and Live a Conscious Life* (Carlsbad, CA: Hay House 2016), xxii.

195 **Kallayil says, "The most important technology every single:** Gopi Kallayil, "Connect with Your 'Inner-Net': Living and Working with Purpose," November 19, 2015, https://knowledge

.wharton.upenn.edu/article/connect-with-your-inner-net-living
-and-working-with-purpose/.

196 **Arianna Huffington makes space for joy:** Arianna Huffington,
"Preventing Burnout and Recharging Your Batteries, *Bulletproof
Blog,* January 31, 2017, https://blog.bulletproof.com/preventing
-burnout-recharging-batteries-arianna-huffington-384/.

200 **We've discussed the negativity bias we all share:** Rick Hanson,
*Buddha's Brain: The Practical Neuroscience of Happiness, Love, and
Wisdom* (Oakland, CA: New Harbinger, 2009).

200 **However,** *as we approach our sixties and beyond*: Laura L.
Carstensen, *A Long Bright Future: Happiness, Health, and Financial
Security in an Age of Increased Longevity* (New York: Broadway
Books, 2009), 5.

201 **According to psychologist Laura Carstensen,** *the sweet spot for our
happiness*: Laura L. Carstensen, Bulent Turan, Susanne Scheibe,
Nilam Ram, Hal Hirshfield, Gregory R. Samanez-Larkin, Kathryn
P. Brooks, and John R. Nesselroade, "Emotional Experience
Improves with Age: Evidence Based on over Ten Years of
Experience Sampling," *Psychology and Aging* 26, no. 1 (2011):
21–33, cited in Hagerty, 139n24.

201 **Carstensen says, "When people face endings they tend to
shift . . .":** Deborah Netburn, "The Aging Paradox: The Older We
Get, the Happier We Are," *Los Angeles Times,* August 24, 2016,
https://www.latimes.com/science/sciencenow/la-sci-sn-older-people
-happier-20160824-snap-story.html.

201 **Research across life spans shows midlife and beyond:** Barbara
Bradley Hagerty, *Life Reimagined: The Science, Art, and
Opportunity of Midlife* (New York: Riverhead Books, 2017), 5.

201 **As Barbara Hagerty says, "I have come to believe that
the forties, fifties, and sixties . . .":** Hagerty, *Life Reimagined,* 4–5.

201 **Hagerty also points out that, historically:** Hagerty, *Life Reimagined*, 22.

202 **As Hagerty explains, "[We] are more likely . . .":** Hagerty, *Life Reimagined*, 5.

202 **As neuroscientist Richard Davidson says:** Barbara Bradley Hagerty interview of Richard Davidson, in Hagerty, *Life Reimagined*, 235.

202 **Developmental psychologist Bernice Neugarten makes a distinction:** Bernice L. Neugarten, "Age Groups in American Society and the Rise of the Young-Old," *Annals of the American Academy of Political and Social Science* 415, no. 1 (1974): 187–198; Bernice L. Neugarten et al., *Personality in Middle and Late Life: Empirical Studies* (New York: Atherton Press, 1964).

202 **Mary Pipher, in *Women Rowing North*:** Mary Pipher, *Women Rowing North* (New York: Bloomsbury, 2019), 1, 3.

204 **The first practice is called "Time for Kindness":** Kristin Neff, *Self-Compassion: The Proven Power of Being Kind to Yourself* (New York: HarperCollins, 2011).

206 **In her decades of work with tens of thousands:** Tara Brach, "The RAIN of Self-Compassion," https://www.tarabrach.com /selfcompassion1/; *Radical Compassion: Learning to Love Yourself and Your World with the Practice of RAIN* (New York: Penguin Press, 2019).

207 **This brings us to the "N" of RAIN which in some versions:** Brach, "The RAIN of Self-Compassion," https://www.tarabrach.com /selfcompassion1/; *Radical Compassion*.

INDEX

The author acknowledges permission to reprint the following:

"The Guest House" from *The Essential Rumi, New Expanded Edition*, trans. Coleman Barks (San Francisco: HarperOne, 2004).

"Love After Love" from *The Poetry of Derek Walcott, 1948–2013* by Derek Walcott, selected by Glyn Maxwell. Copyright © 2014 by Derek Walcott. Reprinted by permission of Farrar, Straus and Giroux.

"Inner Critic Practice" and "Mini-meditations": excerpted from *Real Happiness: The Power of Meditation*. Copyright © 2011 by Sharon Salzberg. Used by permission of Workman Publishing Co., Inc., New York. All Rights Reserved.

"Fluent" from *Conamara Blues: Poems* by John O'Donohue. Copyright © 2001 by John O'Donohue. Reprinted by permission of HarperCollins Publishers.

"To Manage" from *Voices in the Air* by Naomi Shihab Nye. Text Copyright © 2018 by Naomi Shihab Nye. Used by permission of HarperCollins Publishers.

"Seven Key Features of Presence" and "The 3-Minute Breathing Space": John Teasdale, Mark Williams, and Zindel Segal, *The Mindful Way Workbook: An 8-Week Program* (Guilford Press, 2014). Adapted with permission of Guilford Press.

John O'Donohue quote from "Awakening the Mind Workshop" taught by John O'Donohue and Daniel J. Siegel, the Berkshires, Massachusetts, 2006.